OFFICIAL GUIDE TO THE SMITHSONIAN

NATIONAL MUSEUM OF AFRICAN AMERICAN HISTORY & CULTURE

OFFICIAL GUIDE TO THE SMITHSONIAN

NATIONAL MUSEUM OF AFRICAN AMERICAN HISTORY & CULTURE

SMITHSONIAN BOOKS
WASHINGTON, DC

CONTENTS

Preceding page: The latticework of the museum's façade, called the Corona, creates a dramatic view on the second-floor landing.

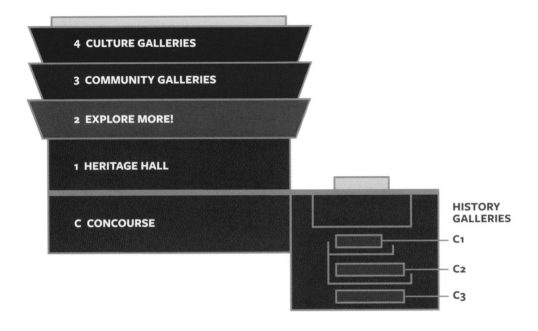

4 CULTURE GALLERIES

3 COMMUNITY GALLERIES

2 EXPLORE MORE!

1 HERITAGE HALL

C CONCOURSE

HISTORY GALLERIES

C1

C2

C3

WELCOME TO THE MUSEUM

It gives me great joy to welcome you to the National Museum of African American History and Culture. As the nineteenth Smithsonian museum, and the newest landmark on the National Mall, we stand among other revered institutions, monuments, and memorials in the nation's capital that commemorate and celebrate the American experience. Looking at the building today, with its distinctive angled silhouette echoing the slanted capstone of the Washington Monument, it seems as if this museum was always meant to be here. As if it simply, finally, claimed a space that was intended for it all along.

In reality, the journey to build the National Museum of African American History and Culture was no easy path. At times it seemed like this museum would never be more than a dream. But for those who believed, the dream was always there, a beacon to keep striving for. Today, this dream is made of concrete, steel, and glass. It is clad in thousands of bronze-colored filigree panels that shimmer against the sky and transform the daily track of the sun into an exquisite dance of shadow and light. It welcomes millions of visitors from across the country and around the world to enter its grand, soaring spaces, to marvel and ponder over the precious artifacts and works of art displayed in its galleries. Today, we can all see and experience the dream that so many pursued for so long.

But there is another dream, one that is about more than building a museum dedicated to African American history and culture on the National Mall. That dream depends not on what treasures are kept inside the museum, but on what our visitors take away with them. That dream is embedded in the museum's mission—to be a place that welcomes all people to learn about how the African American experience has shaped this nation, and to be a place for all Americans to gain a fuller understanding of where we have been, and how we have reached this point in our collective journey, so that we can better move forward, together, toward a future that fulfills our founding promises of freedom, equality, and justice for all.

With the opening of the National Museum of African American History and Culture, the foundation for this dream has been laid. It is now up to all of us to keep on building.

Lonnie G. Bunch III
Founding Director
**National Museum of African
American History and Culture**

The Washington Monument, as seen from the north side of the museum.

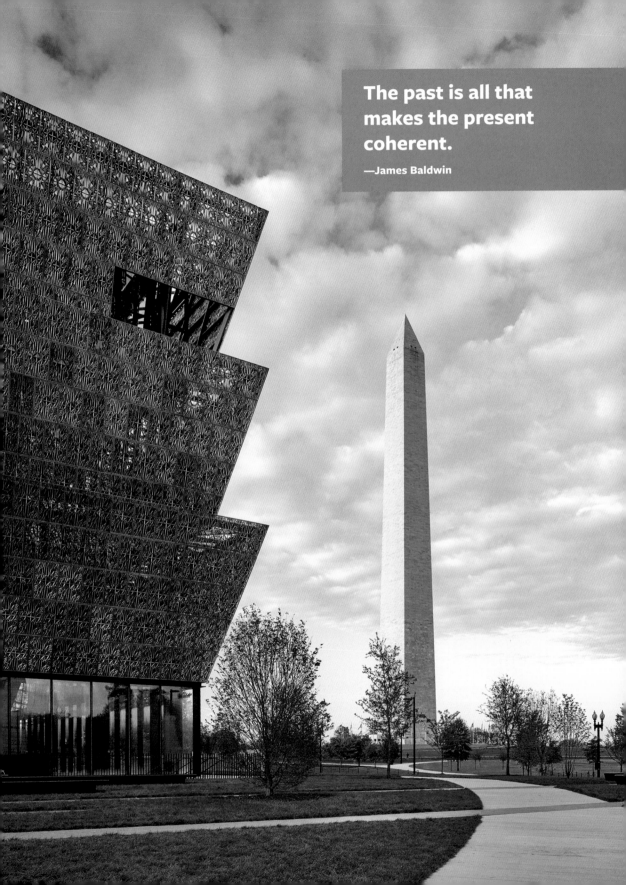

> **The past is all that makes the present coherent.**
>
> —James Baldwin

It is a monument, no less than the others on this Mall, to the deep and abiding love for this country, and the ideals upon which it is founded. For we, too, are America.

—PRESIDENT BARACK OBAMA

A PEOPLE'S JOURNEY, A NATION'S STORY

On September 24, 2016, thousands gathered on the National Mall in Washington, D.C., to witness history in the making—the dedication of the Smithsonian's National Museum of African American History and Culture. This event, celebrated around the world, marked a new chapter for the Smithsonian and for the nation. For the first time, African American history and culture would be presented on a national scale, as a central part of the nation's story. In providing an opportunity for all to discover and revel in this history, the museum would also serve as a vital lens through which to explore and understand what it means to be American.

The journey to build the National Museum of African American History and Culture took numerous steps to realization, including the passage of federal legislation, construction of a majestic new building, and the collection of thousands of artifacts and works of art. It involved the efforts of presidents and members of Congress, curators and architects, art collectors and army veterans, and countless other American citizens. The fulfillment of a long-held dream, it is also the story of an idea whose time has come.

President Obama speaks at the dedication of the National Museum of African American History and Culture, September 24, 2016.

A CENTURY IN THE MAKING

Fifty years after the end of the Civil War, veterans gathered in Washington, D.C., to mark the occasion with a grand parade and encampment on the National Mall. Among those who marched were African American soldiers who had proudly fought under the Union flag. But by 1915, the cause these men had fought for—to end slavery and secure freedom and equal citizenship—had been eclipsed by racial discrimination, including the passage of segregation laws, the horrors of lynching, and the denial of voting rights. "We are sometimes led to ask what has been gained by the Civil War," commented the Baltimore *Afro-American*, one of the country's leading black newspapers, in an editorial about the discriminatory treatment of black veterans. "What has these fifty years brought of fame or honor to them that they might feel proud that they once wore the uniform and fought for a grateful country?" (See page 175.)

Hoping to address this inequity, in 1916 a "Committee of Colored Citizens" launched a campaign to honor the contributions of African American soldiers. The group, which had organized a grand banquet and reception for black veterans during the 1915 encampment, established the National Memorial Association, Inc., to advocate for the construction of a National Negro Memorial in Washington, D.C. In 1923, the association unveiled a new design for the proposed memorial building, a colonnaded marble edifice that would include "a National Hall of Fame, Art and Music Rooms, Library and Reading Rooms, Auditorium seating 5,000, Museum, and space for tablets from the several states to commemorate the men and women of our Race whose deeds entitle them to honorable mention." (See page 175.)

After years of lobbying and fundraising, in 1929 the National Memorial Association succeeded in persuading Congress to approve a joint resolution to "create a commission to secure plans and designs for and to erect a memorial building ... in the city of Washington, as a tribute to the Negro's contribution to the achievements of America." (See page 175.)

President Calvin Coolidge signed the resolution into law on his last day in office. Members of the planning commission, appointed by President Herbert Hoover, included Mary McLeod Bethune, Mary Church Terrell, architect Paul Revere Williams, and other leaders in the fields of business, religion, and education. But a lack of financial support from Congress, combined with the onset of the Depression, prevented the museum project from ever getting off the ground. In 1933, President Franklin D. Roosevelt abolished the memorial planning commission and transferred its duties to the Interior Department, where the project quietly disappeared into the dustbin of bureaucracy.

Supporters used souvenir coin banks like this, ca. 1926, to raise funds for the proposed National Negro Memorial in Washington, D.C.

Right: View of the Contemplative Court, located on the Concourse level.

NED...TO WORK AND FIGHT
NS DOWN LIKE WATER AND
S LIKE A MIGHTY STREAM.

LUTHER KING JR 1955

I CHERISH MY OWN FREEDOM DEARLY,
BUT I CARE EVEN MORE FOR YOUR FREEDOM.

NELSON MANDELA 1991

Local and National Efforts

While the national memorial authorized by Congress in 1929 failed to materialize, other organizations and institutions took up the charge of studying, preserving, and displaying African American history and culture. During the 1950s and 1960s, a new wave of interest in black history and community activism associated with the Civil Rights and Black Power movements led to the opening of African American museums in cities such as Cleveland, Chicago, Detroit, and Boston. These museums, built and supported by private interests, saw their primary responsibility as educating African Americans about their heritage and countering the negative, marginalized, or absent representations of black history and culture in public museums and school textbooks.

By the late 1960s, however, as the country grappled with racial divisions, civil unrest, and other political crises, some began to revive the idea of a museum of African American history and culture that would be designed to serve a broader, national audience—to educate white Americans as well as black Americans. In 1968, Congress held hearings on a proposed bill to establish a National Commission on Negro History and Culture, which would explore the idea of creating a national museum. Among those who testified in favor of the bill were officials of the NAACP, baseball legend Jackie Robinson, television journalist Mal Goode, and author and activist James Baldwin. In his testimony, Baldwin addressed the need for white America to learn about African American history:

If we are going to build a multiracial society, which is our only hope, then one has got to accept that I have learned a lot from you and a lot of it is bitter, but you have a lot to learn from me and a lot of that will be bitter. That bitterness is our only hope. That is the only way we get past it.... It is our common history. My history is also yours.

The bill proposed in 1968 did not go forward in Congress. But the idea of a national African American museum was picked up by lawmakers from Ohio, who believed the appropriate place for such an institution was in Wilberforce, site of the nation's oldest private historically black university. After years of effort, the National Afro-American Museum and Cultural Center opened in 1988. Though national in scope, the Wilberforce museum was not federally funded or authorized. And it was not located where many believed a national museum of African American history and culture needed to be in order to have the strongest impact—in the nation's capital, Washington, D.C.

Sustaining the Dream, 1980s–1990s

In the mid-1980s, a new campaign to establish a national African American museum in Washington, D.C., began to take shape. This effort, initiated by businessman Tom Mack, was championed in Congress by Rep. Mickey

The Smithsonian Arts and Industries Building, considered as a potential site for the new African American museum, is depicted in this pin, ca. 1995.

Leland of Texas, who succeeded in securing passage of a bill to "encourage and support" the raising of private funds to build a museum on federal land. In 1988, Rep. John Lewis of Georgia introduced a bill in Congress to create a National African American Heritage Museum and Memorial as part of the Smithsonian Institution. A renowned veteran of the Civil Rights Movement, Lewis took up this new cause with characteristic passion and determination. For the next thirteen years, he would continue his legislative efforts to establish a national African American museum, working with fellow Democrats as well as Republicans to build bipartisan support.

Prompted by this activity, officials at the Smithsonian began to explore the idea of establishing a new museum. This included appointing a blue-ribbon commission to study the state of African American museums across the United States as well as the representation of African American history and culture at the Smithsonian. In 1991, after a two-year investigation led by Claudine Brown, the African American Institutional Study Commission affirmed the need for a national museum dedicated to African American history and culture. Noting that there "exists no single institution devoted to African Americans which collects, analyzes, researches, and organizes exhibitions on a scale and definition comparable to those of major museums devoted to other aspects of American life," the commission concluded that the best place for such a museum would be at the Smithsonian, on the National Mall. It recommended the Arts and Industries Building as a temporary location for the museum, until a larger, permanent facility could be constructed. (See page 175.)

The National African American Museum Project, directed by Claudine Brown from 1990 to 1995, was established at the Smithsonian to identify potential collections and develop exhibition and programming plans for the new museum.

The Time Has Come, 2001–16

With the Smithsonian on board, it was now up to Congress to approve and authorize the creation of the museum. As is often the case in Washington, however, that was much easier said than done. After ten years of blocked and stalled legislation, a breakthrough finally came in 2001. A bipartisan coalition from the House and Senate, led by Rep. John Lewis (Georgia), Rep. J. C. Watts Jr. (Oklahoma), Sen. Sam Brownback (Kansas), and Sen. Max Cleland (Georgia), succeeded in passing a bill to establish a presidential commission that would develop a plan of action for building the museum. In April 2003, the commission released its report to the president and Congress under a title that aptly summarized the feelings of all who had pursued this effort for so long: *The Time Has Come.*

On December 16, 2003, President George W. Bush signed Public Law 108–184, which established the National Museum of African American History and Culture as the nineteenth museum of the Smithsonian Institution. The legislation stated that the museum "would be dedicated to the collection, preservation, research, and exhibition of African American historical and cultural materials, reflecting the breadth and depth of the experience of individuals of African descent living in the United States." It directed the Smithsonian Board of Regents to appoint an advisory council to help hire a museum director, identify a site for the museum, develop plans for collecting, programs, and exhibitions, and lead efforts to raise the private funds for construction that would be required to match the federal appropriation.

The next several years marked a series of milestones for the new museum. Lonnie Bunch, a historian who had served as associate director of curatorial affairs at the Smithsonian National Museum of American History and president of the Chicago History Museum, was appointed founding director in 2005. One of his first acts

Members of the presidential commission join President Bush for the signing of legislation creating the museum, December 16, 2003.

as director was to convene a scholarly advisory committee to help shape the intellectual agenda, exhibition content, and programming for the museum. The committee, chaired by eminent historian John Hope Franklin until his death in 2009, included leading scholars of history, religion, visual and performing arts, anthropology, education, and other disciplines. Also in 2005, the museum acquired its first donated object, and the massive task of building a national collection of African American history and culture got underway. Over the next decade, the collection would grow from one to nearly 37,000 objects, thanks to generous donations from individuals, families, and organizations and strategic collecting efforts by the curatorial staff.

In 2006, Smithsonian officials announced the selection of the site for the museum, a five-acre parcel adjacent to the Washington Monument,

at the corner of 14th Street and Constitution Avenue, NW. In 2009, Freelon Adjaye Bond/ SmithGroup was selected as the architectural team to design the building, and in 2011 Ralph Appelbaum Associates was awarded the contract to design the museum's eleven permanent exhibition galleries. On February 22, 2012, a groundbreaking ceremony was held at the site, attended by President Barack Obama, First Lady Michelle Obama, Rep. John Lewis, Gov. Sam Brownback, former First Lady Laura Bush, and other distinguished guests.

With ground broken, the engineering and construction crews got to work—digging the museum's 70-foot-deep foundation, building barrier walls to keep the high water table at bay, and pouring the concrete. In November 2013, the museum installed its first exhibition objects, a Jim Crow-era railroad passenger car and a guard tower from Angola Prison in Louisiana, which had to be lowered into the open foundation by crane so the building could be constructed around them. Two years later, in a special event to celebrate the completion of the museum's iconic exterior structure, the building was wrapped with a dynamic projection of photographs, words, and music representing 150 years of African American history and culture.

As the construction of the interior spaces was completed, the exhibition teams moved in to start installing the cases, graphics, hardware, and approximately 3,000 artifacts that had been selected for the inaugural exhibitions. More than 100,000 square feet of empty gallery space gradually filled and came to life with images and stories of African American history and culture. Designers, fabricators, media producers, collection managers, conservators, and curators worked to pull together the finishing touches

and ensure that everything was ready for the grand opening.

And then, finally, suddenly, it was time. On September 24, 2016, staff, volunteers, and supporters gathered to welcome the first official visitors into the museum. A century in the making, the dream that began with a committee of citizens seeking a place of honor for African American veterans in the capital of the nation they had helped to build and defend, the dream that was revived and carried forward by veterans of the Civil Rights Movement, at last culminated with the ringing of a ceremonial bell by Barack Obama, the nation's first black president. The sound of the Freedom Bell, brought to Washington, D.C., from the historic First Baptist Church in Williamsburg, Virginia, signaled that the doors to the National Museum of African American History and Culture were now open to all, a gift to the nation, for present and future generations.

Words from a Civil War recruitment broadside written by Frederick Douglass are projected onto the museum's façade during the "Commemorate and Celebrate Freedom" event in 2015.

LAYING THE FOUNDATION

Donated to the museum in 2011, this ticket from a segregated movie theater in the 1950s is a small but poignant reminder of daily life during the Jim Crow era.

When the National Museum of African American History and Culture opened on the National Mall in September 2016, it was indeed a historic moment. Although the museum now had a permanent home, it had already been up and running for years. Long before the building was designed and constructed, museum staff began collecting artifacts, conducting research, producing exhibitions, educational programs, and publications, forging partnerships with communities and organizations, and developing a digital presence. This work laid the foundation for what was to come, enabling the museum to define its mission and develop its institutional identity, and also cultivated the public support and momentum that were critical to completing the building project.

Collections

At the heart of the museum's mission are the collections, providing a tangible connection to the past and evoking the people, places, moments, and ideas that defined and shaped the African American experience. Unlike many museums, the National Museum of African American History and Culture was not founded on an existing collection. In order to tell the stories it was created to tell, the museum had to seek out and acquire objects that would bring these stories to life. Since 2005, the museum has collected nearly 37,000 artifacts, some 3,000 of which are on display in the exhibition galleries. Many of these objects have been acquired through the generosity of individuals, families, and organizations, who offered their treasured possessions and heirlooms as gifts to the nation. The museum's collection encompasses a wide range of object types, from fine art and photography to manuscripts, musical instruments, clothing and textiles, tools and equipment, and various types of memorabilia. Artifacts also range widely in size, from hatpins, coins, and campaign buttons to a railroad passenger car, a biplane, a Cadillac, and a log cabin. In addition to physical artifacts, the collection includes born-digital materials, such as artwork and photography created in digital format. A skilled team of registrars, collection managers, catalogers, conservators, and digital asset managers cares for the museum collections in the exhibition galleries and at onsite and offsite storage facilities.

Exhibitions

The National Museum of African American History and Culture's exhibitions transform museum objects into tools for learning, props for storytelling, touchstones for remembering, and sparks for discussion. They combine traditional artifact displays with multimedia presentations and interactive and immersive experiences to provide new perspectives on the African American story. In addition to the permanent exhibition galleries, which are broadly devoted to the themes of history, community, and culture, the museum also presents temporary exhibitions in its 4,300-square-foot special exhibitions gallery on the Concourse level, and in smaller gallery spaces in the Earl W. and Amanda Stafford Center for African American Media Arts (CAAMA) on the second floor and the *Visual Art and the American Experience* exhibition on the fourth floor. Prior to the opening of the building, the museum developed a series of temporary exhibitions that were hosted in a special gallery at the Smithsonian National Museum of American History. Several of these exhibitions also traveled to venues across the country, and explored topics such as the history of Harlem's famous Apollo Theater, slavery at Thomas Jefferson's Monticello plantation, and the anniversaries of the 1863 Emancipation Proclamation and the 1963 March on Washington. Many temporary and traveling exhibitions are the product of collaborative partnerships with other institutions, organizations, and local communities, who work with museum staff to develop and tell these stories.

Research

Research informs and supports the curatorial work of the National Museum of African American History and Culture, from collecting artifacts to producing exhibitions, programs, and publications. Museum staff engage also in special research projects to advance the state of knowledge in various fields. Major efforts have included the African American Legacy Series, a multiyear collaboration with Smithsonian Folkways Recordings devoted to exploring African American oral and musical traditions, from blues and gospel to hip-hop and spoken word; the Slave Wrecks Project, an international, multi-institutional, interdisciplinary partnership dedicated to recovering the complex history of the Transatlantic Slave Trade; the Civil Rights History Project, a partnership with the Library of Congress to collect and preserve first-person accounts of the Civil Rights Movement; and the Freedmen's Bureau Project, in which the museum joined with the National Archives and the genealogy organization FamilySearch to index and make records from this Reconstruction-era government agency freely accessible to online researchers. In addition to these projects, the museum has established research centers, programs, and initiatives on topics including African American religion, media arts, oral and family history, and cultural, political, and social intersections between African Americans and other racial and ethnic groups.

View of the museum building from the northeast corner of Constitution Avenue and 14th Street NW at dusk.

Education and Public Programs

Through education and public programs, the museum's collections and research become more accessible and exciting to a diverse local, national, and international audience. Since 2007, the National Museum of African American History and Culture has produced a rich array of public programs, ranging from film screenings, author talks, and panel discussions to musical and theatrical performances, craft demonstrations, and fashion shows. Signature programs and events have included the annual Black History Month Family Day, the Save Our African American Treasures program, which has visited cities across the United States to educate the public about preserving their personal material culture, and the History, Rebellion, and Reconciliation symposium exploring contemporary issues of race and social justice.

While public programs provide educational opportunities for families and lifelong learners, the museum also offers learning activities and resources designed especially for teachers and students, including workshops on teaching and talking about race in the classroom, live classroom videoconferences exploring museum objects and stories, and initiatives to engage learners of different age groups. Enrichment programs for early childhood learners promote positive identity development and provide resources for parents, caregivers, and educators.

Everyone Makes a Difference, a classroom program for children ages four to seven, uses children's literature, touchable objects, and reproductions of artwork to prompt students to think about the different tools people use to make the world better—from speeches to gavels to paintbrushes—and to consider how they can make a difference in their own world. The Power of the Written Word: Teen Writing and Literature Institute, a program for rising 9th through 12th-grade students, uses classic works of African American literature to inspire teen participants to

investigate, discuss, and reflect on major themes explored throughout the museum. The education department also manages a large team of highly trained docents, student interns, and other volunteers who play an essential role in inspiring and engaging museum audiences and supporting behind-the-scenes work.

Office of Strategic Partnerships

Collaboration is a founding principle of the National Museum of African American History and Culture and central to fulfilling its institutional mission. Through the Office of Strategic Partnerships, the museum cultivates professional alliances with African American museums, museums of the African diaspora, and other organizations dedicated to the study of African American history and culture. This work is conducted on local, regional, national, and international levels and involves the sharing of knowledge and resources to mutually advance the missions of the museum and its partner institutions. Through such collaborations, which have included organizations such as the Association of African American Museums (AAAM) and the International Council of African Museums (AFRICOM), as well as other Smithsonian partners, the museum has produced symposia and conferences, supported critical research projects, promoted professional development and institutional best practices, and engaged with African diaspora communities.

The Digital Museum

As a museum born in the twenty-first century, the National Museum of African American History and Culture has "grown up" using information technology and digital content to fulfill its mission and connect with audiences both inside and beyond its walls. On the museum's website, nmaahc.si.edu, you can view thousands of objects from the collections, learn about exhibitions and programs, access educational resources, and plan your visit. You can also download the NMAAHC Mobile App, which will help you navigate the museum and discover stories from the exhibitions and collections. In the exhibition galleries and the Explore More! interactive gallery on the second floor, digital technology helps you experience African American history and culture in new and exciting ways—from sitting at an interactive lunch counter to learn more about civil rights sit-ins, to stomping your feet in a virtual step show. And by following the museum on social media, you can get inside scoops about exhibitions and collections, virtually attend public programs, and participate in a vibrant online community devoted to African American history and culture.

The NMAAHC Mobile App offers behind-the-scenes stories from the museum's exhibitions and collections.

Save Our African American Treasures

We encourage people to become aware of what they have, to protect it and to preserve it so the story of the African diaspora in this country can be told.

—LONNIE BUNCH,
Museum Director

A convention badge, ca. 1920s, worn by a sales agent for Madam C. J. Walker beauty products, was brought to a Treasures event in Chicago in 2008.

Through its signature outreach program, Save Our African American Treasures, the National Museum of African American History and Culture collaborates with cultural institutions and community leaders to educate the public about the importance of preserving African American material culture. The program, launched in 2008, brings curators and conservators into local communities to help individuals identify and care for their treasured family photographs, papers, textiles, and other cultural artifacts. During the first program series, which traveled to fifteen cities across the United States, thousands of keepsakes were brought out from attics and basements to be examined by museum experts.

From hand-stitched quilts, infant christening gowns, and family Bibles to athletic trophies, high-school diplomas, and love letters, these everyday mementoes tell the stories of families and communities and document the richness and diversity of the African American experience. By raising awareness about the value of family heirlooms, and providing information about how to properly store and care for them, the program aims to ensure that these treasures—and the precious histories they contain—will continue to be preserved and passed down to future generations. Some objects shared at these events were later donated to the museum, while others have found homes in local and regional institutions.

To learn about upcoming events and get tips for preserving your own African American treasures, visit the museum's website at nmaahc.si.edu/explore/initiatives/african-american-treasures.

Discovered in an old trunk and passed down as a family heirloom, this 1865 photograph was brought to a Treasures event in Topeka, Kansas, in 2010.

Another treasure from Topeka, this engraved dinner chime from the mid-twentieth century was presented to railroad porter Leo LaRue in honor of his retirement.

RISING UP

RISING UP
THE MUSEUM BUILDING

The National Museum of African American History and Culture presents the story of the United States through the African American lens. This mission, to provide a new perspective on the national experience, is embedded in the form of the building itself. Rising between the Washington Monument and the National Museum of American History, the museum stands alongside the other grand structures on the National Mall, in harmony with its monumental surroundings. But its striking design, defined by the bronze-colored, three-tiered Corona, also announces a distinctive presence: independent, proud, resilient, and triumphant. Just as the building has shifted and reshaped the view of the national landscape, it promises a transformative experience for the visitor.

View of the museum building, looking southeast from the corner of 15th Street and Constitution Avenue, NW.

A SYMBOLIC SITE

The decision to locate the museum on the National Mall, which has long functioned in popular and political culture as the nation's "front yard," affirms and supports the view of African American history and culture as central to the American story. Through its prominent visual relationship to the Capitol and the Lincoln Memorial along the Mall's east-west axis, and to the White House, Washington Monument, and Jefferson Memorial on the north-south axis, the museum is symbolically positioned as part of a national conversation.

The choice of such an eminent site prompted an extensive effort to ensure that the design and construction of the building would harmonize with the historic, aesthetic, and environmental character of the surrounding landscape. Under a process known as Section 106 of the National Historic Preservation Act (16 U.S.C. 470f), which provides rules and regulations for the protection of federal historic resources, numerous experts and members of the general public spent five years studying the issues and identifying solutions. As part of this process, archaeologists also conducted excavations of the site to ensure that no important historical resources were present or disturbed. The final design of the museum building and grounds, which cooperates with the environment while introducing a unique and dynamic element to the National Mall, is a product of this collaborative effort.

This building will stand next to the monument to our first president, George Washington—a man who fought for liberty and who came to recognize the evils of bondage, freeing his slaves in his will. Side by side, these two spots are symbolic of our own national journey. For the stories that will be preserved within these walls ... are the stories of African Americans. But they're also stories that are forever woven through the heart of the fabric of our nation.

—Laura Bush, speaking at the museum's groundbreaking ceremony, 2012

Aerial view of the museum site, looking southwest toward the Washington Monument and Tidal Basin.

THE CORONA

The museum's distinctive three-tiered form, known as the Corona, is an evocative symbol of traditions, influences, and ideas that have defined and shaped the African American experience. In designing the upward-angled shape of the Corona, the architects drew inspiration from the crown-like forms atop wooden architectural columns carved by Olowe of Ise, a Yoruba sculptor of the early 1900s, as well as images of people lifting their arms toward the sky in praise or jubilation, a gesture common to cultures of Africa and the African diaspora. The three levels of the Corona are set at the same seventeen-degree angle as the tip of the Washington Monument, a structure that adopts its own form from ancient Egyptian obelisks.

The Corona is comprised of 3,523 bronze-colored cast-aluminum panels, which form an intricate, gleaming envelope around the five-story glass and steel structure of the museum building. The filigree pattern of the panels is inspired by ornamental ironwork made by enslaved and free African American craftsmen in southern cities, such as Charleston and New Orleans. The varying thickness and opacity of the Corona panels regulate the amount of light and heat entering the building and represent one of the many environmentally sustainable elements incorporated into the museum's design. Around the exterior, cutaways and "lenses" in the Corona provide dramatic views for museum visitors and preserve the historic vistas of the National Mall. One of the largest and most spectacular views, the Mall Panorama, is located on the fourth floor outside the Culture Galleries.

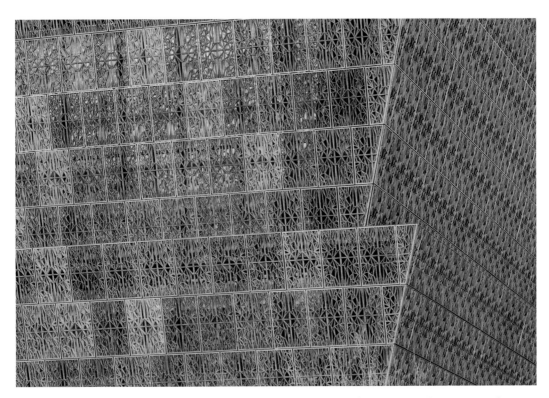

Detail of the Corona, showing the 230-ton façade, which is supported by horizontal trusses that wrap around the building and form three angled tiers.

The first brilliant crop of crocuses emerges on the north lawn while the museum is still under construction in early 2016.

LANDSCAPE

Like the building, the surrounding landscape is thoughtfully designed to resonate with key elements of African American history and culture and to reinforce fundamental themes of resilience, celebration, and uplift.

Entering on the north side from Constitution Avenue, two major features serve as landmarks. The Oculus, a large circular structure near the entrance, functions as the skylight for the Contemplative Court, which is located below ground on the Concourse level. To the west of the Oculus is The Walt Disney Company Reading Grove, an outdoor seating area with benches designed to resemble two clasped hands. The native plantings on the north side of the museum are accentuated by approximately 400,000 crocuses that bloom every February in celebration of Black History Month and as a seasonal symbol of hope and renewal.

The museum's south plaza is designed to provide a welcoming experience for visitors approaching from the National Mall and to serve as a transitional threshold for the journey to come. The porch, a covered area outside the entrance, not only offers shade and shelter, but also represents a historical and cultural space that people throughout the African diaspora have used for family and community gatherings, socializing, storytelling, and sharing lessons. Below the porch canopy is a reflecting pool, which creates a cooling microclimate as breezes pass over the water, refreshing the air. The presence of the reflecting pool at the entrance to the museum symbolizes the crossing of water as a powerful element in the African American experience—from the Atlantic Ocean crossed by enslaved Africans during the Middle Passage, to the biblical River Jordan that marked the Israelites' passage from slavery to freedom, the entrance to the Promised Land.

HERITAGE HALL

Both main entrances on the north and south sides of the museum open onto Heritage Hall. Spanning the entire ground floor, offering sweeping views in all directions through its glass walls, this welcoming entry space is both grand and intimate.

The interior views of Heritage Hall are equally stunning, with works of contemporary art by Chakaia Booker (*The Liquidity of Legacy*, 2016) and Sam Gilliam (*Yet Do I Marvel*, 2016) adorning the walls and a dramatic welded bronze sculpture by Richard Hunt (*Swing Low*, 2016) suspended from the ceiling. Near the escalators is the Walmart Welcome Center, where you can get all the information needed to plan your visit. The Robert Frederick Smith Family Corona Pavilion, a 60-seat theater, provides space for group orientations, special events, and public programs. The museum shop is also located on this level.

From Heritage Hall, a curving monumental staircase leads down to the Concourse level. You can also use the escalators or elevators to access the Concourse, as well as the galleries on the second, third, and fourth floors. Atrium spaces on the west and north sides of Heritage Hall are open all the way to the top floor and offer dramatic views of the intricately designed Corona that envelops the building.

Heritage Hall, looking north toward the Constitution Avenue entrance. Chakaia Booker's sculpture, *The Liquidity of Legacy*, hangs on the east wall.

CONCOURSE

When you see the National Museum of African American History and Culture from the street, you may not realize that you are only seeing half of the museum. In addition to the five floors that rise above the National Mall inside the three-tiered Corona, the building extends another 60 feet below grade. The first of the four lower public levels, the Concourse, is directly below Heritage Hall and can be accessed by taking the monumental staircase at the north end of the hall, or the elevators or escalators.

The Concourse level is where you will go to enter the David M. Rubenstein History Galleries—three exhibitions that chronicle the African American experience over the course of 600 years of history. Adjacent to the entrance to the History Galleries is the Contemplative Court, one of the signature spaces of the museum. Centered around a waterfall that cascades down from a circular skylight, enclosed by amber-colored glass walls that glow like a beacon above the History Galleries, the Contemplative Court offers a place to sit and reflect, to recharge, and to draw inspiration from the words of historical figures, including Martin Luther King Jr., Nelson Mandela, and journalist and activist Frances Ellen Watkins Harper. The space is named in honor of John Hope Franklin, historian and founding chairman of the museum's scholarly advisory committee.

Across from the History Galleries and the Contemplative Court is the entrance to the Oprah Winfrey Theater, a state-of-the-art, 350-seat auditorium that offers film screenings, theatrical performances, lectures, and other public programs. A large special exhibitions gallery is also located on the Concourse level and features temporary exhibitions on various topics related to African American history and culture. Near the entrance to the changing gallery is an exhibit about the history, design, and construction of the museum, *A Century in the Making*, which also features a rotating display of recently acquired objects. A large tapestry by Romare Bearden (*Reflection Pool*, ca. 1975) adorns the wall of the Bill & Melinda Gates Foundation Concourse Atrium.

The Concourse is also where you will find Sweet Home Café, the museum's spectacular homage to African American food traditions. Serving stations offer cuisines from different American regions, including the North States, the Agricultural South, the Creole Coast, and the Western Range. In the seating area, exhibits along the wall explore the history and culture of African American foodways. Through the dishes it serves and the stories it tells, Sweet Home Café illustrates and celebrates the significant contributions of African Americans to the creation and shaping of American food culture.

The curving monumental staircase, supported only at the top and bottom, is an elegant engineering marvel.

HERITAGE HALL
FLOORPLAN

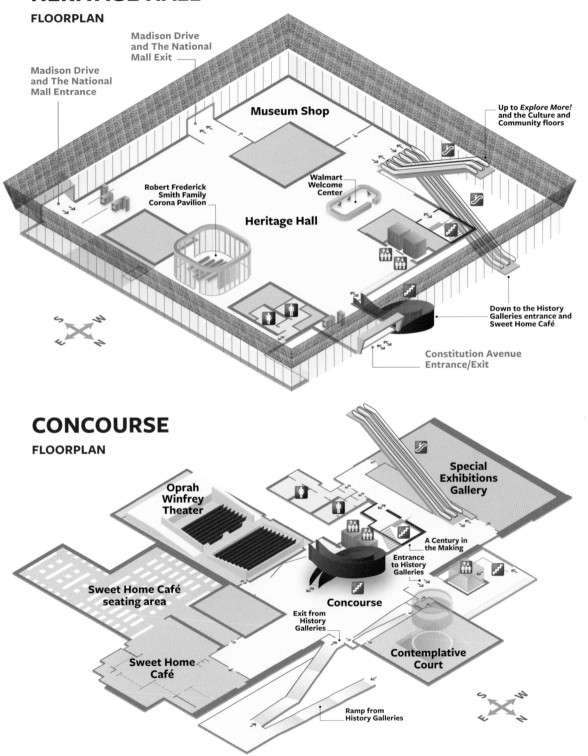

Madison Drive and The National Mall Exit

Madison Drive and The National Mall Entrance

Museum Shop

Up to *Explore More!* and the Culture and Community floors

Robert Frederick Smith Family Corona Pavilion

Walmart Welcome Center

Heritage Hall

Down to the History Galleries entrance and Sweet Home Café

Constitution Avenue Entrance/Exit

CONCOURSE
FLOORPLAN

Oprah Winfrey Theater

Special Exhibitions Gallery

A Century in the Making

Entrance to History Galleries

Sweet Home Café seating area

Concourse

Exit from History Galleries

Sweet Home Café

Contemplative Court

Ramp from History Galleries

Recipes from

Sweet Home Café

Located on the Concourse level, Sweet Home Café offers a menu that showcases a variety of African American food traditions and influences. Here are two delicious recipes you can try at home, courtesy of Executive Chef Jerome Grant and Supervising Chef Albert Lukas of Restaurant Associates.

Chef Jerome Grant serves as the Executive Chef of Sweet Home Café.

THOMAS DOWNING'S NYC OYSTER PAN ROAST

This rich seafood dish is inspired by the renowned abolitionist Thomas Downing, a New York City oysterman, tavern owner, and operator of an Underground Railroad stop.

SERVES: 4 PEOPLE

- 2 dozen shucked oysters, such as Wellfleet or Blue Points, plus ½ cup oyster liquor
- ⅛ cup white wine
- 1 shallot, finely minced
- 3 tablespoons ketchup-based chili sauce, such as Heinz
- 2 tablespoons Worcestershire sauce
- ½ teaspoon celery salt
- ½ stick unsalted butter
- ⅔ cup heavy cream
- Pinch smoked paprika
- Salt to taste
- Ground white pepper to taste
- 12 slices of French bread, cut ½ inch thick
- 2 tablespoons butter

In a medium-sized stainless-steel saucepan, combine the white wine and shallots and bring to a simmer for 1 minute. Add to the wine all of the reserved oyster liquor, chili sauce, Worcestershire sauce, celery salt, and ½-stick butter, and simmer for another 2 minutes. While the sauce is simmering, lightly butter the sliced French bread and bake in a preheated 375 degree oven for approximately 4 minutes until crisp and golden.

Reduce the heat on the sauce to a low simmer. Add the shucked oysters to the sauce and gently simmer for 3 minutes. Add the heavy cream to the oyster sauce and simmer another 3 minutes until the oysters are gently cooked. Be sure not to overcook the oysters as they will curl up and shrink. Remove the pan from the heat.

FINISHING THE OYSTER PAN ROAST

Add the pinch of smoked paprika and season to taste with salt and pepper. Place three slices of bread in the base of each soup bowl and top with six oysters per person. Ladle a generous amount of sauce over each bowl and enjoy!

GULLAH STYLE HOPPIN' JOHN

Hoppin' John, the traditional New Year's Day lunch, is served in our restaurant daily. Black-eyed peas are replaced with Sea Island red peas to create an authentic Gullah version.

SERVES: 4 TO 5 PEOPLE

RICE
4 cups water

1 teaspoon kosher salt

1 teaspoon cayenne pepper

1 cup Carolina Gold rice

1 bunch scallions, thinly sliced

RED PEAS
1 quart chicken stock

2 slices slab bacon cut ⅛ inch thick

½ cup Sea Island red peas (soaked overnight in cold water)

1 cup onions, small diced

½ cup carrots, small diced

¾ cup celery, small diced

2 bay leaves

1 sprig thyme

2 sprigs parsley

COOKING THE PEAS

In a medium-sized saucepot, heat the chicken stock to a simmer along with one slice of the bacon. Drain the peas from the soaking water and add to the simmering chicken stock. Add the remaining ingredients and simmer for approximately 1 hour until tender.

COOKING THE RICE

Bring the water to a simmer along with the cayenne pepper and salt. Add the rice and cook gently over low heat for approximately 20 minutes.

FINISHING THE HOPPIN' JOHN

While the rice is cooking, cut the remaining slice of bacon into strips approximately ⅛ inch wide. Fry the bacon until crisp and transfer to a plate lined with a paper towel to drain excess fat. Using a slotted spoon, remove the peas from the cooking liquid and place into a serving bowl. Gently mix the rice and peas until well blended. Season to taste with salt and pepper. Top with crispy bacon and sliced scallions and serve.

Sweet Home Café, which has seating for 400, welcomes visitors for lunch daily from 11 a.m. to 3 p.m.

HISTORY

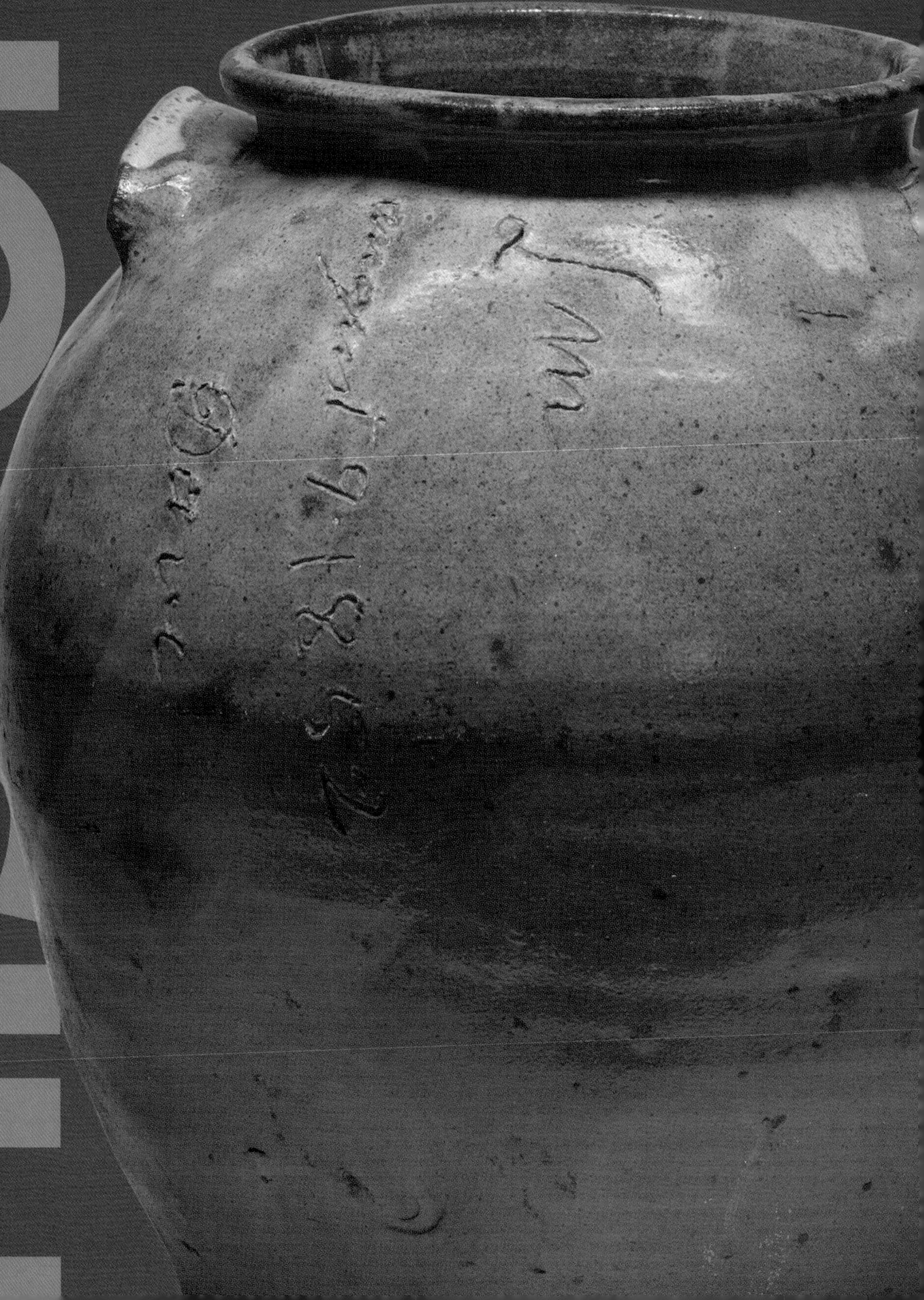

THE DAVID M. RUBENSTEIN HISTORY GALLERIES

THE JOURNEY TOWARD FREEDOM

 C3 **SLAVERY AND FREEDOM**

 C2 **DEFENDING FREEDOM, DEFINING FREEDOM: THE ERA OF SEGREGATION 1877–1968**

 C1 **A CHANGING AMERICA: 1968 AND BEYOND**

Literally and symbolically, the History Galleries serve as the foundation upon which the National Museum of African American History and Culture stands, and this is where you are encouraged to begin your journey through the museum. The entrance to the History Galleries is located on the Concourse level. A large observation window overlooks the monumental, 60-foot-high space, in which three exhibitions, layered one atop the other and connected by a series of ramps, traverse through 600 years of history.

To start your journey, take the large glass elevator down to *Slavery and Freedom*, located on the lowest level of the History Galleries. You will then proceed upward through time, passing through *The Era of Segregation* and ending with *A Changing America*. Upon leaving the History Galleries, you may wish to visit the Contemplative Court to spend some time in quiet reflection before returning to the Concourse level.

Storage jar made and signed by David Drake, commonly known as "Dave the Potter," an enslaved man in South Carolina, 1852.

American history is longer, larger, more various, more beautiful, and more terrible than anything anyone has ever said about it.

—JAMES BALDWIN

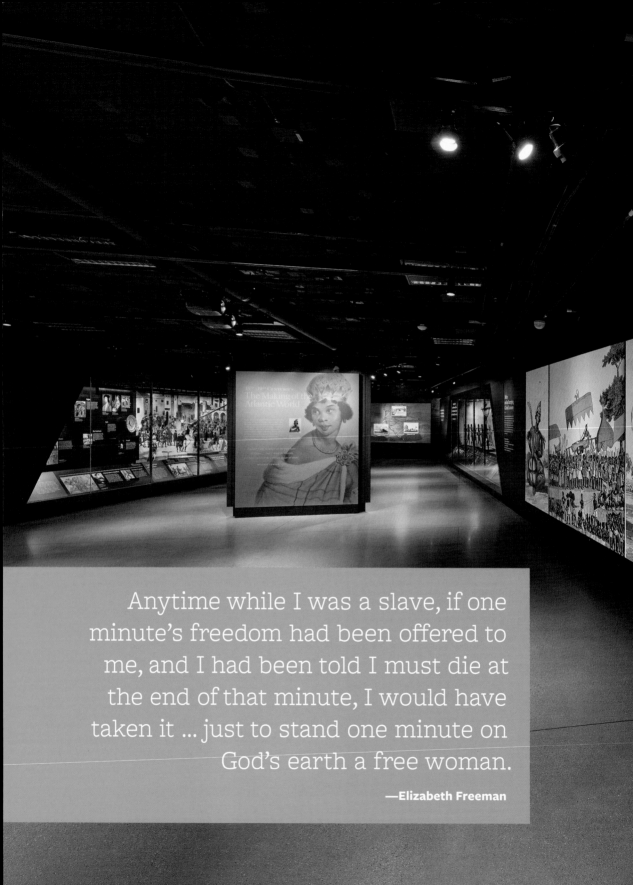

Anytime while I was a slave, if one minute's freedom had been offered to me, and I had been told I must die at the end of that minute, I would have taken it ... just to stand one minute on God's earth a free woman.

—Elizabeth Freeman

Slavery
&Freedom
1400-1877

Five hundred years ago, a new form of slavery transformed Africa, Europe, and the Americas. For the first time, people saw other human beings as commodities—things to be bought, sold, and exploited to make enormous profits. This system changed the world.

The United States was created in this context, forged by slavery as well as a radical new concept, freedom. This is a shared story, a shared past, told through the lives of African Americans who helped form the nation.

*We've got t
the unvarnish*

JOHN HOPE FRAN

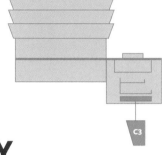

C3

SLAVERY AND FREEDOM

Five hundred years ago, the emergence of the Transatlantic Slave Trade transformed Africa, Europe, and the Americas. People treated other human beings as commodities—things to be bought, sold, and exploited to make enormous profits. This system changed the world.

The United States was created in this context, forged by slavery as well as a radical new concept, freedom. *Slavery and Freedom* explores the complexity of this story, which rests at the core of Americans' shared history. Through powerful objects and first-person accounts, it examines slavery from the perspectives of those who experienced it—the enslaved and the enslavers, those who supported and profited from the system, and those who fought to abolish it. As the exhibition considers the central role that slavery played in the making of the United States, it also reveals the ways in which the actions of ordinary men and women, demanding freedom, transformed a nation.

Slavery and Freedom begins by tracing events in Africa and Europe that gave rise to the global slave trade.

SLAVERY AND FREEDOM

Slavery and Freedom is located on level C3, which is accessible via elevator and stairway from the entrance to the History Galleries on the Concourse level. The exhibition covers 400 years of history, from the rise of the global slave trade, to the founding of the United States, to the Civil War and Reconstruction.

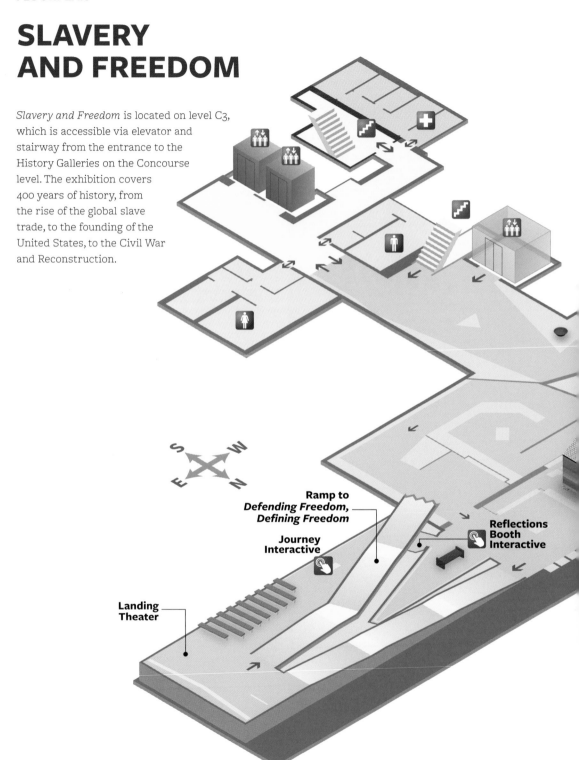

Ramp to
Defending Freedom,
Defining Freedom

Reflections
Booth
Interactive

Journey
Interactive

Landing
Theater

Lobi amulet in the form
of miniature shackles,
1600s–1700s

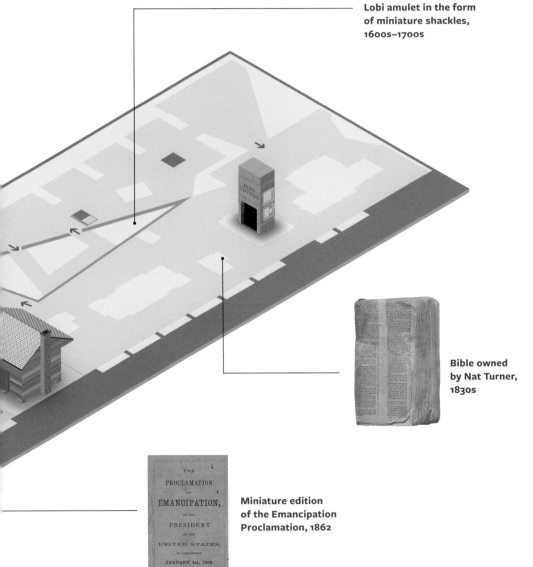

Bible owned
by Nat Turner,
1830s

Miniature edition
of the Emancipation
Proclamation, 1862

The Making of the Atlantic World, 1400–1865

In the 1400s, national boundaries did not exist as they do today. People across western Africa and Europe gradually came into closer contact and exchanged goods, cultures, and knowledge. Part of this trade included enslaved people—an ancient practice around the globe. People and places connected throughout the Atlantic rim made up the Atlantic world. By the 1600s, an unanticipated shift took place. A new form of slavery took hold, and the primary commodity became enslaved African people.

As you enter the *Slavery and Freedom* exhibition, an introductory video provides a glance into the varied peoples, kingdoms, and cultures that existed throughout the continent of Africa before the acceleration of trade with Europe. Beyond the entrance, two parallel cases running along the walls examine the converging cultural, political, and economic forces in Africa and Europe that gave rise to a new global economy. In this context, massive profits and a callous disregard for human life fueled the Transatlantic Slave Trade and built European nations. Objects include European maritime navigation tools used by sailors to reach the western African coast;

examples of trade goods exchanged between Africans and Europeans, including beads and rifles; and a bronze plaque from the Benin Kingdom depicting African emissaries who negotiated with Europeans seeking to trade in gold, spices, textiles, and literature. A large sugar pot symbolizes the new commodity that, starting in the late 1500s, became the primary driver of the Transatlantic Slave Trade.

An iron pot, used to boil down sugarcane, rests on a pile of sugar. By 1787, 90 percent of the world's sugar was produced by enslaved Africans in the Caribbean.

The Middle Passage, 1514–1866

The vast profit to be gained, along with the high mortality rate of enslaved people on plantations, pulled a steady stream of captives from the African interior. This trade stripped kidnapped Africans of their rights and freedom, resulting in a new form of slavery that treated humans as property—chattel slavery. For approximately 440 years, European trade companies shipped

15ᵀᴴ–19ᵀᴴ CENTURIES

The Middle Passage

A Full Complement of Negroes

For four centuries, slavers sailed along the western African coast to pack the hulls of their ships with "a full complement of negroes." Millions of captive Africans were loaded onto slave ships as commodities certain to bring a profit. The traumatic journey from western Africa to the Caribbean and the Americas—known as the Middle Passage—was a mixture of captivity and commerce. Enslaved Africans were dispersed throughout the Atlantic world and forced to leave their homeland and loved ones behind.

West African Adinkra symbols of freedom and captivity are juxtaposed on this wall with the names of slave ships.

over twelve million enslaved Africans from the western coast of Africa to the Caribbean and the Americas. This traumatic journey, known as the Middle Passage, linked Africa, Europe, and the Americas in a way that forever changed the globe. Enslaved Africans were sold in exchange for goods like cloth and gunpowder and to labor on sugar and tobacco plantations in the New World. On the Middle Passage journey, captive Africans aboard slave ships faced an unknown future away from home and family, and were subjected to violence, disease, and starvation. Many enslaved people rebelled, both aboard slave ships and in the New World. Others chose suicide, jumping into shark-infested waters rather than enduring the horrors of enslavement. While many souls were lost during the Middle Passage, those who survived did so through courage, strength, and the will of the human spirit.

The Middle Passage story in *Slavery and Freedom* begins with a video, "The Last Footfall,"

presenting the perspective of an enslaved African about to embark on this forced journey across the Atlantic, never to return. Printed on the walls surrounding the screen are the names of hundreds of slave ships and the numbers of enslaved Africans that they carried, many of whom perished during the voyage. Doorways lead into a darkened space, designed to evoke the hold of a slave ship, where artifacts and voices provide a powerful and poignant reflection on the brutality of the Middle Passage and pay tribute to those who endured this experience. Among the objects on view in this sacred space are relics recovered from the *São José-Paquete de Africa*, a Portuguese slave ship that wrecked off the coast of South Africa in 1794 with hundreds of enslaved Africans aboard; iron shackles used to restrain men, women, and children during the long and brutal weeks of the Middle Passage; and a tiny protective amulet in the shape of shackles, attributed to the Lobi people.

The Transatlantic Slave Trade, 1514–1866

The Transatlantic Slave Trade was the largest forced migration of people in world history. Profits from the sale of enslaved humans and their labor laid the economic foundation for Western Europe, the Caribbean, and the Americas. The human cost was the immense physical and psychological toll on the enslaved. Their lives were embedded in every coin that changed hands, each spoonful of sugar stirred into a cup of tea, each puff of a tobacco pipe, and every bite of rice. Objects that symbolize the economic profits and human costs of the Transatlantic Slave Trade include a British two-guinea coin, minted with gold generated by slave labor and bearing the elephant and crown emblem of the Royal African Company; a whip likely used on enslaved West Africans who labored under brutal conditions on New World plantations; and a first edition of the autobiography of Olaudah Equiano, whose compelling personal account of his journey from slavery to freedom helped to mobilize support for the abolitionist cause.

Enslaving Colonial North America, 1565–1776

Of the more than twelve million enslaved Africans transported to the Americas, approximately 400,000 came to the present-day United States.

In the Carolina Lowcountry, enslaved Africans forged a distinctive culture that emphasized kinship and community.

When Africans arrived, they found themselves in different physical and social environments. They asserted new identities, created their own cultures, and resisted enslavement, while contributing to the physical, cultural, and intellectual foundations of colonial North America. But as West Africans (such as the Yoruba, Igbo, Kongo, and Fon) began remaking themselves as African Americans, European colonists instituted new laws that defined them as something else: "black." These laws supported the transformation of the American system of slavery into an institution that was race-based, lasted for life, and was inherited from one generation to the next.

Slavery and Freedom explores the different experiences of slavery in four geographical regions: the Chesapeake, the Carolina Lowcountry, Louisiana, and the northern colonies. Artifacts that help to tell these stories include tools used for tobacco cultivation in the Chesapeake, where an early interracial workforce of enslaved Africans, European indentured servants, and American Indians gradually shifted to an African workforce that was enslaved for life; a fanner basket from Senegal, which represents the knowledge of rice production brought by enslaved West Africans that transformed South Carolina into one of the richest colonies before the Revolution; and a copy of the Code Noir, a 1685 decree by France's King Louis XIV that regulated the practice of slavery in French Louisiana and granted enslaved people the right to appeal against mistreatment by slaveholders. Also on view is a group of small items—cloth, pins, beads, glass, and a cowrie shell—found under the attic floorboards of a colonial-era home in Newport, Rhode Island. Believed to be a nkisi, a bundle of objects created to hold and transmit spiritual power, it suggests how enslaved Africans in northern colonies found ways to maintain and practice their cultural beliefs, even within the confined quarters of slaveholders' homes.

The Revolutionary War, 1775–83

The Revolutionary War was waged for independence from Britain in the name of equal rights for men, while nearly one-fifth of the colonial population was enslaved. This contradiction, inherent from the beginning of the nation, escalated black revolutionary thought and action. For Africans, the Revolution was primarily about another kind of independence—freedom from slavery. Though slavery continued, enslaved people seized the opportunity to support the efforts of colonists or the British, based on which side they believed would guarantee them freedom.

Highlights in this section include an immersive setting that re-creates the scene of the 1770 Boston Massacre in which Crispus Attucks, a fugitive from slavery, was killed as he led an interracial group of fellow sailors in a confrontation with British troops. Attucks, the first casualty of the American Revolution, became a legendary symbol of American patriotism, heroism, and resistance. Overlooking the scene is an illustrated timeline of the Revolution that lists major events along with personal stories of black people, free and enslaved, who fought for their freedom on both sides of the conflict.

Also on display is a powder horn that commemorates Prince Simbo, an African American who served as a private with the 7th Regiment, Connecticut Line of the Continental Army. After Simbo was mustered out in 1787, the people of his hometown of Glastonbury voted to award him a plot of land in honor of his patriotic service.

Powder horn, late eighteenth century, carved with the name of Prince Simbo, a Continental Army soldier.

THE
SLAVE
WRECKS
PROJECT

Just to be able to dive that site, to find a tangible piece of artifact, or information, something to raise their silent voices, to tell their story, is an extraordinary thing. —KAMAU SADIKI, volunteer and lead instructor, Diving With a Purpose

Maritime archaeologists document the site of the *São José* shipwreck off the coast of Cape Town, South Africa.

Iron ballast block from the wreck of the slave ship *São José*, photographed in situ.

On December 27, 1794, a Portuguese slave ship bound for Brazil carrying 512 captives from Mozambique sank in a storm off the coast of Cape Town, South Africa. Approximately half of the Mozambicans were rescued from the foundering ship, only to be resold into slavery after reaching shore. The remaining captives perished in the waves.

For two centuries, the fateful voyage of the *São José-Paquete de Africa* remained buried and lost to history, along with the wreckage of the ship itself. But through the efforts of the Slave Wrecks Project (SWP), a research and education initiative launched in 2008, this and other lost histories of the global slave trade are being recovered. A collaboration hosted by the National Museum of African American History and Culture, with core partners from The George Washington University, the U.S. National Park Service, Iziko Museums of South Africa, and Diving With a Purpose, SWP supports an international team of maritime archeologists, historians, educators, and cultural heritage preservationists, who work to locate and document sunken slave ships around the world in order to help tell the story of the global slave trade and its enduring legacies. In 2011, Iziko maritime archaeologist Jaco Boshoff discovered the captain's account of the 1794 sinking of the *São José* in the archives of the Dutch East India Company in Cape Town. The description matched the location of a shipwreck found by treasure hunters in the 1980s, which had been identified as a Dutch vessel. Through a series of investigations conducted at the site and in archives in South Africa, Portugal, the Netherlands, and Mozambique, SWP experts confirmed that this was, in fact, the wreck of the *São José*.

In 2014 and 2015, the first artifacts from the wreck were brought to the sea's surface. They included iron ballasts, commonly used in slave ships as counterweights for the human cargo, pieces of timber and copper fastenings from the ship, and the concretized remains of iron shackles. On June 2, 2015, a ceremony was held at the wreck site to honor the 512 captives aboard the *São José* who lost their lives or were sold into slavery. Community leaders sent soil from Mozambique to be deposited at the site, symbolically returning these lost souls to their native land and bringing their story back into public memory.

The Slave Wrecks Project is continuing to apply and expand its dynamic approach to global public history through further investigations into the voyage of the *São José* and through work at other archaeological sites, in museums and archives, and in classrooms and communities around the world, from Mozambique and South Africa to Senegal and St. Croix. To learn more about the Slave Wrecks Project, visit the museum's website at nmaahc.si.edu/explore/initiatives/slave-wrecks-project, and stop by the Explore More! interactive gallery on the museum's second floor, where you can engage in a virtual exploration of the wreck of the *São José* and analyze artifacts recovered from the site.

Soil from Mozambique, held in this box adorned with cowrie shells, was ceremonially deposited at the wreck site in memory of the captives aboard the *São José*.

Thomas Jefferson, who declared "all men are created equal," also owned 609 slaves during his lifetime.

The Paradox of Liberty, 1776–87

As you move into the next section of *Slavery and Freedom*, for the first time you enter the grand, monumental space that you saw from the overlook point at the entrance to the History Galleries. This transition evokes the sense of freedom that many African Americans believed would be possible with the founding of a new nation based on ideals of equality and democracy. Yet embedded in the foundations of the United States was a troubling paradox—the fight to secure liberty had also secured the perpetuation of slavery.

In this section of the exhibition, the paradox is raised and debated through five historical figures, each presenting a different perspective on the definition of freedom in the era of the American Revolution. The first is Thomas Jefferson, who helped to create a new nation based on individual freedom and self-government. Jefferson stands on the platform against a backdrop of bricks that bears the names of hundreds of men, women, and children he held in bondage. Next to Jefferson is Benjamin Banneker, a self-taught mathematician, scientist, and writer, who participated in the initial land survey of the District of Columbia and published a yearly almanac. In 1791, Banneker corresponded with Jefferson on the issue of slavery and asked him to correct his "narrow prejudices" against Africans. Others on the platform include the poet Phillis Wheatley, who used her literary talents to navigate a society that both enslaved and celebrated her; Elizabeth Freeman, known as Mum Bett, an enslaved woman in Massachusetts who successfully sued for her freedom; and Toussaint Louverture, who led a rebellion on the enslaved French colony of Saint-Domingue (Haiti) that ultimately secured independence and abolished slavery.

Beyond the Paradox of Liberty platform, the monumental Wall of Freedom presents a chronological display of the nation's founding documents, from the Declaration of Independence to the Reconstruction Amendments. Displayed alongside the statements of the founding fathers are the words of African Americans, such as Absalom Jones, Harriet Tubman, Frederick Douglass, and other African Americans, who spoke out against injustice and demanded equal protection under the laws of the land. These powerful juxtapositions illuminate the vital role African Americans played to expand American democratic ideals laid out in the nation's founding documents.

Handmade tin containing a certificate of freedom issued to Joseph Trammell, Loudoun County, Virginia, 1852.

Free Communities of Color

Free blacks lived in North America as early as the 1500s. During the Revolutionary period, slavery's tight grip loosened for some African Americans, allowing the growth of free communities across the new nation. Confronted with racism, inequality, and laws that restricted their rights and liberties, free blacks developed strategies for survival and ways to maintain their freedom. They worked collectively to establish churches, build institutions, and stand in solidarity with their enslaved brothers and sisters. Unable to secure full freedom, some looked to countries outside of the United States, like Liberia and Haiti, as places where African Americans could emigrate to and settle. Among the objects on display that reflect the development of free communities of color are a money box used

Silver teapot made by Peter Bentzon, a free black artisan in Philadelphia, ca. 1817–29.

by Bishop Richard Allen, founder of the African Methodist Episcopal denomination and leader of Mother Bethel A.M.E. Church in Philadelphia; and a teapot made by Peter Bentzon, who was born free in the Caribbean and trained as a silversmith in Philadelphia. He operated shops in Philadelphia and St. Croix in the early to mid-1800s.

Other objects reflect ways in which free African Americans fought injustice, including an original petition signed by Paul Cuffe, an entrepreneur and philanthropist, demanding his right to vote as a Massachusetts taxpayer; and a handmade tin box made by Joseph Trammell of Loudoun County, Virginia, to protect the certificate of freedom he was required by law to carry.

Slavery and the Making of a New Nation, 1790–1861

America's promise of freedom is filled with contradiction. Few people understood this more clearly than enslaved and free African Americans. As the lifeblood of the new republic, slavery expanded with brutal intensity after the Revolution. A federal law prohibiting the importation of enslaved people into the United States took effect in 1808, which paved the way for the development of a massive—and immensely profitable—domestic slave trade. The national economy relied upon slavery, the U.S. Constitution defended slavery, and the country expanded west to extend slavery.

On auction blocks like this one across the United States, enslaved men, women, and children were displayed and sold to the highest bidder.

As you approach this section, a tower of stacked cotton bales looms above you, representing the industry that drove the expansion of slavery in the United States and forced enslaved African Americans to work longer, harder, and faster in order to meet increased production quotas. Next to the tower is a bell from Magnolia Plantation in Cane River, Louisiana, which rang to order slaves to the cotton fields and signaled "weigh-up" time at the end of the day. A field whip represents the brutal methods used by plantation owners and overseers to enforce daily quotas, which could be as much as 300 or more pounds per day. The rise of "King Cotton" also caused the breaking up of families by slave traders to meet the demands for labor in the Deep South. An auction block from Hagerstown, Maryland, where the local sheriff made money by capturing and selling accused fugitives, testifies to the painful and terrifying experiences of men and women treated like property and sold away from loved ones. On the wall surrounding the auction block are names, descriptions, and prices of hundreds of enslaved people, excerpted from bills of sale and other legal documents of the domestic slave trade, bearing silent witness to this system of heartache, profit, and dehumanization.

The lives and labor of enslaved African Americans transformed the United States into a world power. Yet they received no recognition or payment for what they created. By 1860, four million enslaved people produced more than 60 percent of the nation's wealth, and the slave trade valued them at $2.7 billion. This vast wealth, in human form, affected the entire nation. A wall displaying hundreds of bank notes from the antebellum period symbolizes the role of slavery as the foundation of the U.S. economy, driving the development of banking and finance, agriculture, and industrialization —producing the clothing Americans wore, the food they ate, the infrastructure that grew and connected their cities, and the money they earned and invested.

Making a Way: Daily Acts of Resistance

African Americans fought slavery and inequality in ways large and small—from open rebellion to subtle acts of resistance. Using connections—family, neighbors, worship services, and formal political conventions —African Americans shared news, created networks, and developed strategies for "making a way out of no way." State and local governments responded with "black codes" and "slave codes," race-based laws that prohibited African Americans from learning to read and write, practicing their religion, gathering in groups, and engaging in other activities.

One of the fundamental restrictions placed on enslaved people was the denial of their right to marry. And yet, many men and women still exchanged wedding vows and considered themselves husbands and wives. During the 1830s, Rev. Alexander Glennie, Episcopal rector of All Saints Parish, Waccamaw, South Carolina, informally married hundreds of enslaved couples, using an expandable brass wedding ring that he carried with him on his visits to plantations.

Daily acts of resistance—such as exchanging informal wedding vows, learning to read in secret, or gathering to pray in "hush harbors"—undermined slavery and created a measure of freedom. Yet enslaved people also took even greater risks by organizing rebellions or running for freedom. The numbers of those escaping slavery became so remarkable that Americans began to refer to the pathways as the Underground Railroad. Objects that tell such stories include the Bible owned by Nat Turner, the enslaved minister who led a slave rebellion in Southampton County, Virginia, in 1831; and a lace shawl and hymnal owned by Harriet Tubman, who guided hundreds of enslaved people to freedom while working with other antislavery activists on the Underground Railroad.

Renowned antislavery activist Harriet Tubman received this shawl as a gift from Britain's Queen Victoria around 1897.

Life and Work, 1820–65

Despite daily denials of their humanity, enslaved African Americans sustained a vision of freedom by making lives of their own. They built their own identities and created cultures instilled with wisdom, beauty, and vitality. Living a dual life— one of hardship and one of community and faith —enslaved people turned their focus toward family, hope, and joy, wherever it might be found.

The centerpiece of this story, and one of the museum's most significant artifacts, is a slave cabin from the Point of Pines Plantation on Edisto Island, South Carolina. Built around 1853, likely by enslaved carpenters, the cabin served as home to a family who used it to raise children, nurture one another, and build community. In front of

A 150-year-old slave cabin was carefully dismantled, piece by piece, brought to the museum, and reassembled for the *Slavery and Freedom* exhibition.

Point of
Pines Cabin

To Have and To Hold

the cabin, a display of domestic items includes a wooden bowl carved with designs similar to those found in western Africa; a large iron cooking pot; and a stoneware storage jar made and signed by enslaved potter David Drake. However, like many slave cabins, this place of refuge could quickly turn into a site of terror where family members could not protect their own from punishment, sale, or sexual assault.

The double reality of enslavement—the daily violence enslaved people were subjected to and the everyday ways they resisted it—extends from the cabin to an array of objects and images that explores the story of life, work, and enslavement from a variety of perspectives. Among the highlights are a wrought-iron grave marker made by enslaved blacksmith Solomon Williams for his wife, Laide Williams; a skirt carefully pin-tucked by the mother of Lucy Lee Shirley, an enslaved girl in Loudoun County, Virginia; a Bible in which Richard Collins recorded the names and birthdates of his family members after he became free; and a child's cradle, made by an enslaved person, displayed next to a pair of iron shackles. All of these items evoke the deep bonds that African American families forged and the powerful lessons they passed down as they survived generations of enslavement.

The Coming of War, 1820–61

In two generations, cotton produced by enslaved people transformed a fledgling nation into a world power and a leader in global trade. This rapid change sparked heated political debate. Southern slaveholders demanded political power to match their financial influence. Northern interests pushed back, fearing the power of the slave-owning minority. This unease over slavery created dangerous new forms of racism. Together, enslaved and free, African Americans organized to overthrow slavery.

Antislavery: A Movement in Black and White, 1820–61

In the 1820s, African American and white abolitionists began working together to pressure Americans to confront the brutal realities of slavery. Alarmed by the rapid expansion of slavery beyond the Mississippi River, they forged new and unexpected relationships that defied the color line. Abolitionists disagreed on the best tactics for defeating slavery and over the question of what freedom would mean for African Americans. But by uniting around a common cause, a small coalition of people who had little access to political power succeeded in changing America.

Objects that illustrate the development and leadership of the antislavery movement include a collection box used to raise funds for the Rhode Island Anti-Slavery Society; an issue of the *North Star*, the newspaper founded by Frederick Douglass in 1847 to promote abolition and women's rights; and a watch owned by antislavery activist William Lloyd Garrison, publisher of *The Liberator*.

The family of abolitionist William Lloyd Garrison used this coin box, 1830s–50s, to raise money for the cause.

Civil War and the Coming of Freedom, 1861–65

The Civil War was a war about slavery, but not to end slavery. The North was committed to limiting the spread of slavery but hesitant to abolish it; the South was committed to preserving slavery at all costs. When the war began, however, tens of thousands of enslaved African Americans entered Union lines, determined to end slavery by escaping bondage. Black abolitionists and their white allies used the power of the pen to demand emancipation. For African Americans, the Civil War was always a fight for freedom.

The story of the Civil War comes to life in this section through compelling artifacts, such as a Sibley tent used to shelter self-emancipated men, women, and children who sought refuge at camps established by the U.S. Army; a huge, eight-foot-tall recruitment broadside that boldly calls upon "Men of Color" to enlist in the Union army, signed by Frederick Douglass and dozens of other abolitionist leaders; and a diary kept by Lt. John Freeman Shorter, who served with the 55th Regiment of the Massachusetts Volunteer Infantry. This section also features a video about the Civil War and a timeline of key events and personal stories.

Emancipation and the Transformation of America, 1863–77

The Emancipation Proclamation, which declared the freedom of enslaved people living in Confederate states, committed the nation to ending slavery. Yet what would this freedom mean? Economic independence? Freedom from fear? The right to vote? Propelled forward, the nation and the people responded—in courthouses, in legislatures, on farms, and in homes and factories. Reconnecting with family, building new lives, and restoring communities, African Americans vigorously debated and fully embraced freedom.

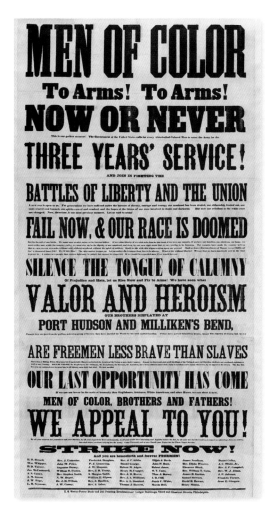

The Union army opened its ranks to black soldiers in 1863. By war's end, an estimated 180,000 African American men had responded to the call.

As you reach this section in the *Slavery and Freedom* exhibition, you once again step out into the grand, soaring space of the History Galleries, an experience that calls to mind the jubilant relief, excitement, and hope that emancipation inspired among African Americans. Displayed in a case at the center of this gallery is a small, handheld copy of the Emancipation Proclamation, printed for Union soldiers to carry and read aloud on plantations and in cities throughout the South.

After the Civil War, from 1865 to 1870, Congress enacted a series of amendments to the U.S. Constitution intended to secure civil rights for African Americans and establish a new foundation of freedom for the nation. Known as the Reconstruction Amendments, they included: the Thirteenth Amendment, which permanently abolished slavery; the Fourteenth Amendment, which granted all citizens equal protection under the law; and the Fifteenth Amendment, which extended voting rights to black men. Early copies of the Emancipation Proclamation and the Thirteenth Amendment, on long-term loan from David M. Rubenstein, are on display in a case along the monumental wall.

After slavery, African Americans expressed and pursued their newly won freedom in many different ways. The people who occupied the cabin on Point of Pines Plantation in South Carolina after 1865 spent time to weatherproof, expand, and personalize their home in ways that slavery had not permitted, as evidenced by the layers of newsprint, magazines, and wallpaper they pasted onto the walls for decoration and insulation, and the back door and new room they built for added privacy. Free to assemble in spaces of their own making, African Americans established institutions for education, religious worship, and social interaction. Many of these grew out of and expanded upon institutions founded by free communities of color during the antebellum period. One example is Metropolitan A.M.E. Church, founded in Washington, D.C., in 1838, which by the 1880s had become one of the most prominent black churches in the nation;

After emancipation, occupants of the Point of Pines cabin added a back door to allow for more freedom of movement.

led by Bishop Daniel A. Payne, its congregation included noted political figures, such as Frederick Douglass and Senator Blanche K. Bruce. A pulpit from Metropolitan A.M.E. Church symbolizes the role of black churches as places of sanctuary, as well as civic engagement and political organization. In addition to exercising their voting rights, many African American men ran for and won political office during the Reconstruction era, including William Beverly Nash, a South Carolina state senator from 1868 to 1877, whose cane and campaign pin are on display here.

At the end of this section, you can read quotations from historical figures who contributed to the struggle to end slavery and secure freedom for all Americans, including Sojourner Truth, Frederick Douglass, Susan B. Anthony, William Lloyd

Formerly enslaved, William Beverly Nash of South Carolina, shown in this pin of ca. 1868, became a prominent politician and businessman during Reconstruction.

Garrison, and Harriet Tubman. You can also visit the Reflections Booth, an interactive recording booth where you can share your own thoughts about what you have seen.

Landing Theater: Reconstruction

Moving up the ramp, you reach the first of three landing theaters that serve as transition points between the exhibitions in the History Galleries. The *Slavery and Freedom* landing theater presents a video about Reconstruction, a period in American history marked by tremendous change and possibility, a time that saw African Americans laying claim to their rights and freedoms as citizens and building institutions to develop and advance black communities. Also in this space, a media interactive, "Journey Toward Freedom," offers an opportunity to explore select themes and stories from *Slavery and Freedom* in more detail.

Freedom never descends upon a people. It is always bought with a price.

—Harry T. Moore

DEFENDING FREEDOM, DEFINING FREEDOM

THE ERA OF SEGREGATION 1877–1968

The years after the Civil War were hopeful and disheartening for African Americans. With the end of slavery, they had hoped to attain full citizenship. Instead, they found themselves resisting efforts to put in place a new form of oppression—segregation. In the face of these attacks, African Americans created institutions and communities to help them survive and thrive. Through their struggle, they challenged the nation to live up to its ideals of freedom and equality.

Defending Freedom, Defining Freedom: The Era of Segregation 1877–1968 spans from the end of Reconstruction through the modern Civil Rights Movement. As you make your way through the exhibition, you will encounter powerful artifacts that testify to the pressures and threats that African Americans confronted during this era, the strength and resilience of African American communities, and the strategies that civil rights activists employed to effect change.

Freedom House: An 1870s' log house built by formerly enslaved African Americans marks the entrance to *The Era of Segregation* exhibition.

DEFENDING FREEDOM, DEFINING FREEDOM:

THE ERA OF SEGREGATION 1877–1968

Defending Freedom, Defining Freedom: The Era of Segregation 1877–1968 is located on level C2, and is accessed via ramps leading up from *Slavery and Freedom* on level C3. The exhibition spans from the end of Reconstruction through the modern Civil Rights Movement.

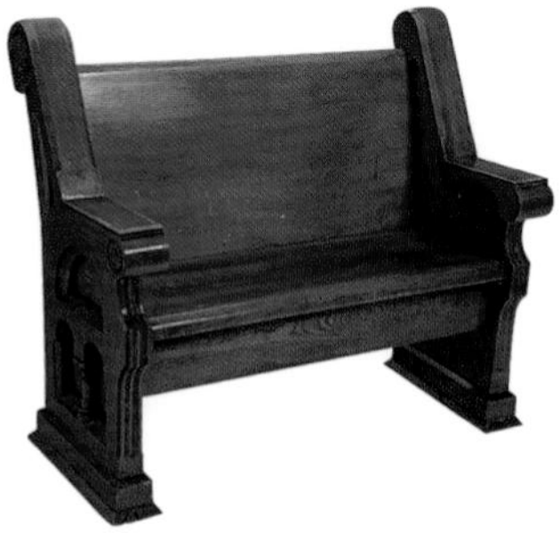

Pew from Quinn Chapel A.M.E. Church, Chicago, 1891

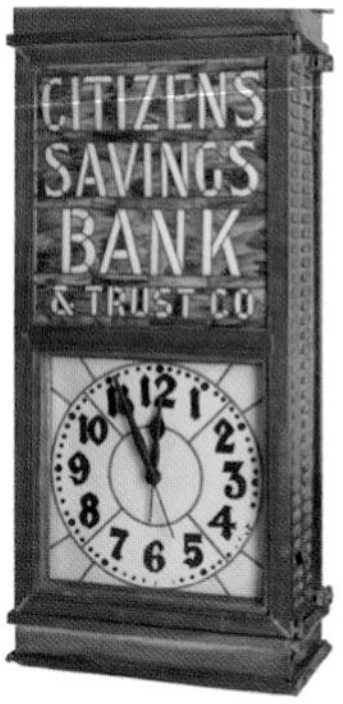

Clock from Citizens Savings Bank and Trust Company, Nashville, 1920–2013

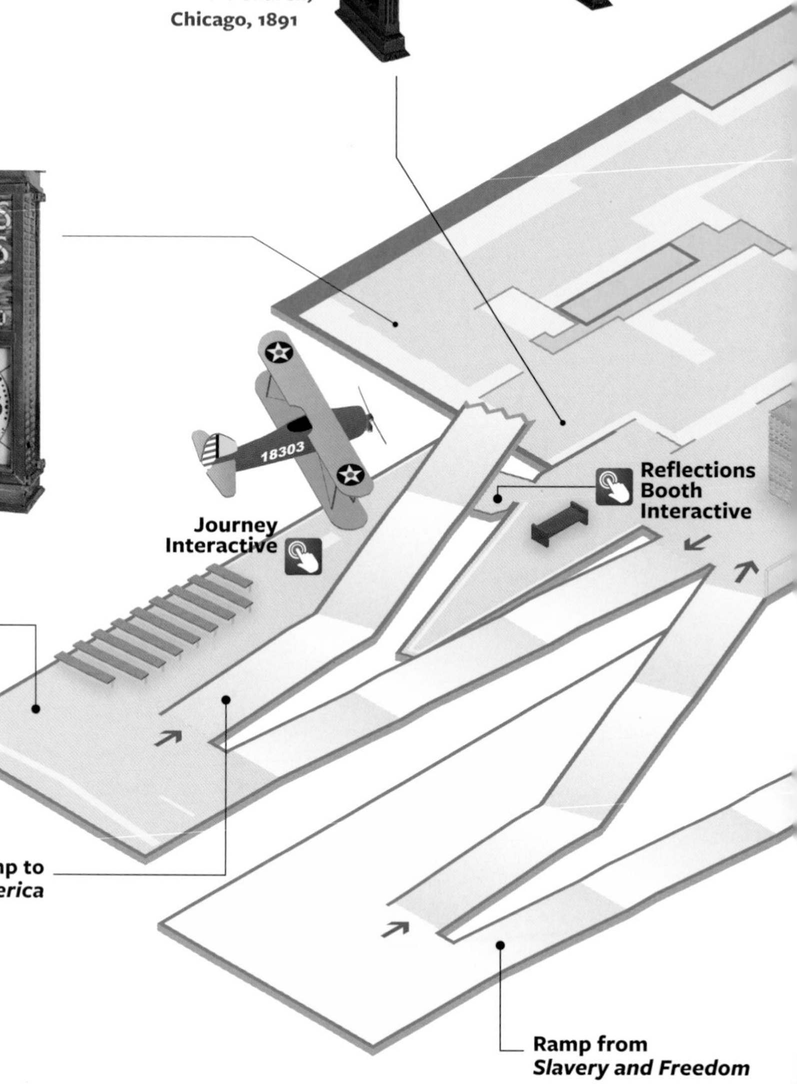

Reflections Booth Interactive

Journey Interactive

Landing Theater

Ramp to *A Changing America*

Ramp from *Slavery and Freedom*

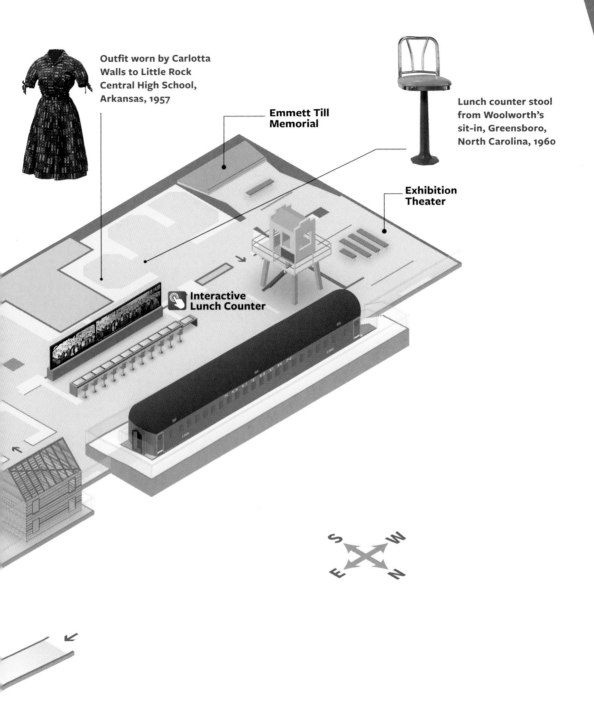

Outfit worn by Carlotta Walls to Little Rock Central High School, Arkansas, 1957

Emmett Till Memorial

Lunch counter stool from Woolworth's sit-in, Greensboro, North Carolina, 1960

Exhibition Theater

Interactive Lunch Counter

S W
E N

Post-Civil War Years

After the Civil War, the federal government controlled the states of the former Confederacy. During this period, known as Reconstruction, federal troops were stationed throughout the South. African Americans made economic progress and elected representatives to local, state, and national governments. But this progress was opposed and undermined by white southerners, who used violence and intimidation to discourage African Americans from voting, owning land, and exercising their independence.

Seeking refuge from this hostility, African Americans created separate towns and neighborhoods in which they were the majority. Here they had greater independence and opportunity to buy land, build churches, and establish schools. The structure that greets you at the entrance to the exhibition, the Jones-Hall-Sims House, is from the community of Jonesville, Maryland, a black settlement founded by brothers Erasmus and Richard Jones on land they purchased from their former enslavers. Built around 1874, this one-and-a-half-story log house represented the Jones family's status as free and independent landowners, in contrast to the one- or two-room cabins they would have occupied during slavery. Step inside to see original furnishings that were kept and used by descendants who lived in the house up through the late 1900s.

Surrounding the Jonesville house are objects and stories from other all-black towns established across the country during this period, from Whitesboro, New Jersey to Nicodemus, Kansas.

Also featured in this opening section are stories of individual African Americans who made efforts to forge a new life for themselves in the years after the Civil War. Born enslaved in Virginia, Clara Brown moved to Colorado after gaining her freedom and became a prominent landowner and community leader. She also spent years trying to locate her children, who had been sold away during slavery, and eventually succeeded in reuniting with one of her daughters. A statue of Brown sits at the entrance to the exhibition. A second statue nearby represents Robert Smalls, a Civil War hero and congressman from South Carolina, who was one of more than 1,400 black men who held political posts during and after Reconstruction. In 1862, Smalls led a group of enslaved African Americans who freed themselves by commandeering a Confederate ship in Charleston Harbor and sailing to the Union fleet. Smalls later returned to his native city of Beaufort and bought the house that had belonged to his former enslavers. An elegant walnut side chair and other furnishings from Smalls's home are on display next to his figure.

Like other Reconstruction-era black politicians, Robert Smalls eventually lost his position as southern Democrats systematically deprived blacks of the right to vote. This was accomplished by a series of laws, known as "black codes," which former Confederate states passed to restrict the civic and economic rights of African Americans. Another form of control was imposed through the sharecropping system, which kept poor African Americans in a permanent state of peonage, unable to own land and control their economic destiny.

Creating a Segregated Society, 1877–1900

When Reconstruction came to an end in 1877, the majority of African Americans lived in the South. As white southerners regained control of state and local governments, they passed new laws to keep blacks and whites segregated and to condemn African Americans to an inferior, second-class citizenship. To resist the impact of these laws, African Americans created communities and institutions to sustain themselves and looked for ways to protest their treatment.

A wall of stereotypical artifacts evokes the racist attitudes African Americans confronted during the Jim Crow era.

Jim Crow Laws

The first part of this section of the exhibition examines the ways segregation became the law of the land throughout the South. After the 1896 *Plessy v. Ferguson* decision by the U.S. Supreme Court upheld the legality of segregation under the doctrine of "separate but equal," segregated streetcars, restaurants, and other public facilities became commonplace. Most often, the facilities reserved for use by African Americans were inferior in quality.

To enforce the segregation laws and prevent African Americans from asserting their rights, white southerners often used terrorism in the form of lynching, rape, and other acts of violence—real and threatened—to create a climate of fear and intimidation. The Ku Klux Klan, organized by Confederate veterans in Tennessee in 1865, quickly spread throughout the South and carried out attacks on African Americans as well as white Republican politicians. While KKK "night riders" wore hoods and robes to appear ghostlike to their victims and avoid identification, other acts of racial violence were conducted in broad daylight and treated as public spectacle, as shown by the popularity of souvenir postcards depicting the lynched bodies of African American men.

Among the leading voices to speak out against the horrors of lynching was Ida B. Wells. Born enslaved in Mississippi in 1862, Wells became a journalist and newspaper editor in Memphis, Tennessee. She traveled through the South, investigated lynching, and wrote a book condemning the practice. Forced to leave Memphis because of her work, Wells lectured internationally against lynching and urged Congress to pass an anti-lynching bill. She also was a forceful advocate for civil rights and women's suffrage. A tea set owned by Wells, which she used when hosting fellow activists at her home, is on display here.

While more intense and visible in the South, discrimination was also part of daily life in the North, where many schools and communities were segregated by race. Popular culture reflected and reinforced white prejudices against African Americans through the use of racist stereotypes. In this section of the exhibition, a case filled with stereotypical artifacts from the late 1800s and early 1900s—from toys and advertisements to tobacco tins and salt-and-pepper shakers—testifies to the prevalence of racist images in everyday American life. Depicting black people as slow-witted, lazy, untrustworthy, and childlike, these caricatures served a common purpose: to justify the logic of segregation and the denial of full citizenship rights to African Americans.

Building Community and Creating Culture

To shield their families from the unfairness of segregation, African Americans created communities that served their social, political, educational, and religious needs. The organizations and institutions they formed—from churches and schools to fraternal groups and literary clubs—provided opportunities to interact with one another and hold positions otherwise denied to them. Among the artifacts to represent these community-building efforts are an oak pew

Women's organizations provided vital support for African American communities. This ca. 1924 banner is from the Oklahoma Federation of Colored Women's Clubs.

from Quinn Chapel A.M.E. Church, the oldest black congregation in Chicago; a grouping of bricks and cornerstones from historically black colleges and universities (HBCUs), including Prairie View A&M University, Bethune-Cookman University, and Spelman College; and a banner from the Oklahoma Federation of Colored Women's Clubs, founded in 1910, which represents the emergence of African American women's organizations during this era. By participating in community activities, African Americans also developed the skills in oration, organizing, and leadership that ultimately served them so well in demanding their rights as citizens. A video in this section, "Debating the Path Forward," examines how three civil rights leaders—educator Booker T. Washington, scholar W. E. B. Du Bois, and journalist Ida B. Wells—framed the political and social issues confronting African Americans and proposed different strategies to overcome racial discrimination.

Given the ways in which popular media depicted African Americans in the decades after the Civil War, many white Americans would have dismissed the idea that African Americans contributed anything important to American culture. But noteworthy African American writers and composers emerged well before 1900. From poet Paul Laurence Dunbar and author Charles Chesnutt to ragtime king Scott Joplin, jazz pioneer Jelly Roll Morton, and the renowned Fisk Jubilee Singers, these artists presented unique perspectives on African American life and created music, verse, and literature with a distinctive style, voice, and rhythm. Their works attained wide popularity and added something entirely new to American culture.

Building National Institutions, 1900–17

In 1903, scholar and civil rights leader W. E. B. Du Bois warned: "The problem of the twentieth century is the problem of the color-line." The solution to that problem would depend largely on how people of color responded to efforts to control and dehumanize them. Excluded by the larger society, African Americans protested inequality and at the same time created institutions, businesses, organizations, and communities to meet their own needs. As the

Henry Long, a Pullman porter in Seneca, South Carolina, purchased this parlor organ for his family in 1911.

African American population enlarged, their organizations increased in size and influence.

Artifacts in this section represent the institutions African Americans created to support their communities and advance the cause of equality during the segregation era. The development of black financial institutions and black entrepreneurship is evoked by items such as a clock from the Citizens Savings Bank, established in Nashville, Tennessee, in 1904 by R. H. Boyd and other local black business leaders; tins for beauty products designed for African American consumers by the Madam C. J. Walker Manufacturing Company; and a pin from the National Negro Business League, launched by Booker T. Washington in 1900 to help create a network of successful black businesses and improve the economic standing of African Americans. The role of the black press as an advocate for community development and racial justice is represented by front pages of black newspapers, including the *California Eagle* and the *Chicago Defender*, while an armchair from Sixth Mount Zion Baptist Church in Richmond, Virginia, bears witness to the ongoing role of religious institutions in providing leadership and support to African American communities.

The development of educational, social, and economic institutions supported the emergence and growth of a new black middle class. Described by W. E. B. Du Bois as the "Talented Tenth," this prosperous segment of African American society consisted of teachers, doctors, lawyers, entrepreneurs, and other professionals who were expected to propel the entire race forward through their examples of success and service. A parlor organ purchased in 1911 by Henry L. Long symbolized the middle-class lifestyle he was able to provide for his family by working as a Pullman porter, a job valued in the African American community for its steady income, elite status, and travel opportunities. Many middle-class African Americans also belonged to social organizations, such as Masonic lodges and Greek-letter fraternities and sororities,

which provided opportunities to develop leadership skills and professional networks. The story of these organizations is explored here through objects such as a badge from the Deborah Grand Chapter Order of Eastern Star, a women's organization affiliated with the Prince Hall Masons; and a silver presentation cup from an Ohio lodge of the Grand United Order of Odd Fellows in America, a fraternal organization founded in 1843 for African American men who were excluded from joining the white Independent Order of Odd Fellows.

Organizing for Equality

As the twentieth century began, African Americans faced increasing violence and still more legislation created to further restrict their rights. The rise of lynching and the outbreak of race riots in cities like Atlanta, Springfield, and East St. Louis occurred in tandem with the expansion of peonage and convict leasing to control black labor, the enforcement of Jim Crow laws to segregate transportation and other public facilities, the use of poll taxes and literacy tests to deny black voting rights, and the introduction of restrictive housing covenants to block African

The NAACP awarded its annual Spingarn Medal for outstanding achievement to Major Charles Young in 1916.

Americans from renting and buying property in white neighborhoods. In response, activists came together to found new national organizations, such as the Niagara Movement, the National Association for the Advancement of Colored People (NAACP), and the National Urban League. They used lobbying, protest marches, and other tactics to fight for equal citizenship rights and seek changes in the way African Americans were treated. The NAACP Spingarn Medal awarded in 1916 to Major Charles Young, the highest-ranking African American military officer at that time, represents that organization's mission to promote equality and fight racial prejudice.

A porter's cap worn by Philip Henry Logan during his career as a Pullman porter on the Southern Railway.

The Great Migration

Between 1910 and 1970, approximately six million African Americans moved from the South to northern, midwestern, and western states in the Great Migration—one of the largest and fastest mass migrations in the nation's history. Drawn largely by new jobs in war industries, the first wave of more than one-and-a-half million people moved during and after World War I, and the second wave during and after World War II. By 1970, more than 80 percent of African Americans lived in urban locations and only a slight majority—53 percent—remained in the South.

This section of the exhibition explores the history of the Great Migration and its impact on African American communities, American culture, and the urban landscape. It illustrates the economic, social, and cultural transitions that African Americans experienced in moving from the rural South to the urban North, from field to factory. It also highlights personal stories of migrants such as Lollaretta Pemberton, a native of Marshall, Texas, who relocated to California after marrying Grover Allen in 1939; her wedding dress and scrapbook are on display here. You can sit and browse interactive scrapbooks that feature additional migration stories of people who moved from the South as well as to the United States from other countries.

Pullman porters, who provided personal service to passengers on the United States railroads, also served as vital sources of information for African American travelers during the Great Migration. Their role is represented here by a display of items, including a porter's cap, ticket punch, and platform stool. Also on view is a desk from the Chicago office of Robert Sengstacke Abbott, founder of the nation's leading African American newspaper, the *Chicago Defender*. By reporting on job opportunities and living conditions in the North, the newspaper helped fuel migration to Chicago and other northern cities. As Pullman porters traveled throughout the South, they secretly shared copies of the *Defender*, which was banned in many southern cities.

The New Negro Steps Forward, 1917–45

The experiences of World War I, at home and abroad, changed the attitudes of a generation of African Americans. They were less willing to retreat in the face of discriminatory treatment. They felt greater pride in their African heritage and grew more strident in their resistance to attacks on their civil rights. This new attitude was evident in their music, literature, and other cultural expressions, as well as in their political and social activism.

World War I: Democracy Abroad, Injustice at Home

When the United States entered World War I, African Americans questioned how much they should support a war "to make the world safe for democracy" when they were deprived of freedom at home. Those who served hoped their loyalty and bravery during the war would prove that they deserved better treatment back home. The service of black soldiers in World War I is represented here by objects such as a Croix de Guerre medal awarded to members of the 369th Infantry Regiment. Because of racial prejudice in the U.S. armed forces against black soldiers performing combat duty, the 369th, known as the Harlem Hellfighters, served under the command of the French Army. In 1918, the French government awarded the entire regiment the Croix de Guerre, its highest military honor, for bravery in combat.

After soldiers returned home, emboldened by their wartime experiences, they were less willing to accept racism. This new confidence, combined with competition for jobs and housing in a depressed postwar economy, triggered resentment among whites and fueled the outbreak of race riots in cities across the United States during the summer and fall of 1919. Racial violence and terrorism continued into the 1920s, as white mobs destroyed African American communities and massacred residents in places like Tulsa, Oklahoma, and Rosewood, Florida. The 1920s also saw the resurgence of the Ku Klux Klan, the white supremacist organization that targeted immigrants and Catholics as well as African Americans. A red robe worn by an officer of the Klan, a photograph of Klan members marching in front of the Capitol in Washington, D.C., and other paraphernalia are displayed here to represent the group's influence.

The New Negro Movement

In 1919, political activist Hubert Henry Harrison launched a newspaper that vigorously protested the lynching and riots taking place across the United States. The name of Harrison's

A handmade banner from the mid-twentieth century endorses Father Divine, spiritual leader and founder of the International Peace Mission, who attracted a worldwide following.

Minds and Attention Love and Devotion Ideas and Opinions All Concentrated on the Fundamental God Father Divine

publication, *The New Negro*, evolved into a broader term meaning racial pride, resistance to oppression, and the rejection of white stereotypes of African Americans. In 1925, writer and philosopher Alain Locke used the title for an anthology of fiction, poetry, and essays by black authors that gave voice to an emerging African American literary, artistic, and cultural movement known as the Harlem Renaissance. A video in this section of the exhibition explores the movement, which flourished not only in Harlem but across the United States in places like Memphis, Chicago, Los Angeles, and Washington, D.C., and introduced the world to the work of writers, musicians, and artists, such as James Weldon Johnson, Langston Hughes, Zora Neale Hurston, Bessie Smith, Duke Ellington, and Jacob Lawrence.

Speaking out against injustice was a vital part of the spirit of the New Negro. A variety of individuals and organizations emerged demanding change and full citizenship for African Americans. While these activists differed in the kind of changes they sought, they were united in the belief that change was needed immediately. Highlights in this section include a hat worn by Marcus Garvey, the Pan-Africanist political leader, journalist, and orator; and jewelry worn by Dorothy Height, a social justice and human rights activist who served as president of the National Council of Negro Women, an organization founded by Mary McLeod Bethune in 1935.

Other objects in this section reflect the emergence of new African American religious movements that offered spiritual as well as political and economic strategies for promoting racial pride and self-determination. These include a miniature Qur'an owned by Elijah Muhammad, leader of the Nation of Islam; and a handmade banner promoting the ministry of Father Divine, a charismatic spiritual leader who offered a philosophy of racial equality and, in his words, "heaven here on earth."

A miniature Qur'an acquired by Nation of Islam leader Elijah Muhammad during a pilgrimage to Mecca in 1959.

The Depression and Discrimination

The economic downturn after 1929 hit African Americans particularly hard. By 1932, roughly half were unemployed. Many public assistance programs gave African Americans less than white people, and some charitable organizations refused to help black families at all. African Americans found themselves pushed out of lower-paying jobs by whites desperate for work. Falling prices for cotton and other crops devastated black sharecroppers, and two-thirds of them made no profit or went into debt.

In addition to economic hardships, African Americans continued to confront racial oppression, injustice, and intimidation throughout the 1930s. Among the objects that reflect this experience is a "Save the Scottsboro Boys" pin, expressing support for nine African American teenagers falsely convicted of rape by an all-white jury in Scottsboro, Alabama, and sentenced to death. With the support of the Communist Party, the boys' case was appealed and ultimately overturned by the U.S. Supreme Court. Also on view is a fragment of rope used to hang Matthew Williams, an African American man who was lynched in Salisbury, Maryland, in 1931; the rope was handed out as a souvenir after the lynching and collected by Paul Henderson, a photographer for the Baltimore *Afro-American* newspaper who reported on the tragedy.

Navigating a Segregated Reality

Segregation did not prevent African Americans from building vibrant communities. They did the same things most Americans did, but not always at the same places or in the same ways. They visited with friends and family, went to the beach, held social functions, and attended church, among other activities. Their separate world provided a safe haven from insults, mistreatment, and violence. African American experiences of travel and recreation during the era of segregation are represented here by an array of images as well as objects, such as a sign from Rock Rest, a bed and breakfast in Maine that catered to black tourists; a "Colored Section" sign from a segregated train car; and a guidebook published by the *Afro-American* newspaper listing friendly accommodations for black travelers.

African Americans and World War II

As they had in World War I, African Americans also served in segregated units throughout World War II. Most worked in support units, driving trucks, maintaining equipment, and delivering supplies. As casualties mounted, they saw combat in Europe and the Pacific. Women also served in segregated units in the Women's Army Corps and the Army Nurse Corps. Black nurses were allowed to aid only African American troops and German prisoners. Despite these segregated conditions, more than 900,000 African American men and women served and earned many wartime honors, including army chaplain Louis Beasley, whose field communion kit is on display here.

The International Labor Defense, the legal arm of the U.S. Communist Party, issued this 1931 button supporting the Scottsboro Boys.

Army chaplain Louis Beasley used this field kit to serve communion to soldiers during World War II.

The nation's entry into World War II, justified as a fight for freedom and democracy, inspired a renewed push by African Americans to secure equal treatment at home. Expressing their hopes for a "Double Victory" against fascism abroad and racism at home, civil rights activists waged campaigns against job discrimination and segregation. A video in this section illustrates how the tactics they used, including court cases, boycotts, picketing, sit-ins, and mass demonstrations, helped to lay the foundation for the modern Civil Rights Movement.

"Freedom Now!" The Modern Civil Rights Movement, 1945–68

After World War II, a generation of African Americans saw less and less reason to endure attacks on their civil rights. Training under the G.I. Bill had lessened African American dependence on sharecropping. Moreover, rising numbers of African Americans relocated to cities. They wanted change immediately and were willing to force change even at the risk of their own safety. Returning veterans and their generation were central to the success of the Civil Rights Movement that emerged after the war.

Displays at the entrance to this section of the exhibition evoke the powerful and menacing forces that confronted African Americans as they prepared to fight for their civil rights. A case filled with stereotypical objects reflects the persistence of racist imagery in popular culture. A door from a San Antonio, Texas, restaurant declares the front entrance to the establishment to be for "Whites Only." A locket holds photographs of Harry and Harriette Moore, Florida civil rights activists who were murdered by white supremacists in 1951.

But the violence and threats intended to deter African Americans from seeking equality only strengthened the resolve of activists. Using a variety of tactics, they organized and launched campaigns to attack Jim Crow laws throughout

People and events of the Civil Rights Movement, including Rosa Parks and the Greensboro sit-in, are highlighted in this gallery.

1966–1967

For all their influence, the Civil Rights Act and the Voting Rights Act did not bring an end to violence against civil rights workers, laws against interracial marriage, or other forms of racial discrimination. The laws also did not halt discrimination in housing. After 1965, activists turned their efforts to changing housing laws, fighting poverty, and improving employment opportunities for African Americans.

Activist Rosa Parks made this dress in 1955–56. Her arrest in 1955 for defying segregation laws sparked the Montgomery bus boycott.

the South. When civil rights workers achieved a victory, such as the breakthrough 1954 U.S. Supreme Court ruling *Brown v. Board of Education*, they braced against the inevitable white backlash, absorbed it, and used that energy and momentum to propel further action.

As you make your way through this section of the exhibition, objects, images, and video take you on a chronological journey through major events of the modern Civil Rights Movement. Milestones of the movement's early years are marked by a collection of artifacts, including a pair of white and black baby dolls used by psychologists Kenneth and Mamie Clark, whose studies of the negative impact of segregation on African American children were used as evidence in the *Brown v. Board of Education* case; a dress made by Rosa Parks, whose refusal to give up her seat to a white passenger on a segregated city bus launched the Montgomery, Alabama, bus boycott in 1955; a skirt and

Fragment of a stained glass window shattered by the 1963 bombing of 16th Street Baptist Church in Birmingham, Alabama.

blouse worn by Carlotta Walls LaNier, one of the nine students who desegregated Little Rock Central High School in 1957; a stool from the Woolworth's lunch counter in Greensboro, North Carolina, where college students staged a successful sit-in protest in 1960; and a denim vest worn by Joan Trumpauer, a white student activist who was jailed in Mississippi for her participation in the 1961 Freedom Rides challenging segregation on interstate buses.

1963

The March on Washington for Jobs and Freedom, held on August 28, 1963, drew more than 250,000 people to Washington, D.C., to participate in a peaceful mass demonstration for racial equality. On the steps of the Lincoln Memorial, Martin Luther King Jr. delivered his historic "I Have a Dream" speech outlining his vision for an integrated American society. Less than three weeks later, on September 15, a bomb planted by white supremacists exploded at 16th Street Baptist Church in Birmingham, Alabama, killing four young girls: Denise

Joan Trumpauer Mulholland wore this denim vest during her years as a civil rights activist in Mississippi.

McNair, Carole Robertson, Addie Mae Collins, and Cynthia Wesley. A case displays shards of stained glass recovered from the rubble of the church, while videos in this section of the exhibition explore the significance and impact of these two watershed events, which generated nationwide attention and support for the Civil Rights Movement.

1964–65

The next two years saw steady strides forward in the struggle for justice and equality along with continued resistance from white segregationists. Activists succeeded in persuading Congress to pass two major civil rights laws: the 1964 Civil Rights Act, which gave the federal government a new role in desegregating schools and other public facilities, restricted the use of literacy tests for voter registration, and created the Equal Employment Opportunity Commission to oversee race and sex discrimination in employment; and the 1965 Voting Rights Act, which outlawed literacy tests, poll taxes, and other obstacles to voting and required special provisions in certain jurisdictions to ensure minority voting rights were protected. Pens used by President Lyndon B. Johnson to sign these two historic pieces of legislation are on display, along with a video documenting the 1965 march from Montgomery to Selma, Alabama, organized by leaders of the Southern Christian Leadership Conference and the Student Nonviolent Coordinating Committee, which helped bolster public support for passage of the Voting Rights Act.

After 1965

For all their influence, the Civil Rights Act and the Voting Rights Act did not bring an end to violence against civil rights workers, laws against interracial marriage, or other forms of racial discrimination. After 1965, Martin Luther King Jr. and other activists shifted their efforts to fighting poverty and improving employment opportunities for African Americans. At the time of his assassination in 1968, King was planning a Poor People's March on Washington, D.C. A tub used by the great civil rights leader to soak his feet after the five-day march from Selma to Montgomery in 1965 is a poignant symbol of his commitment to the long journey to freedom.

At the same time, a new movement was emerging that rejected the nonviolent approach and integrationist goals of earlier civil rights activists in favor of militant self-defense, efforts to secure black control of black communities, and the promotion of black pride. Largely inspired by the messages of Malcolm X, a minister of the Nation of Islam and advocate for black self-determination, the Black Power Movement gained momentum after 1965 through the leadership of activists such as Stokely Carmichael and the formation of the Black Panther Party. A tape recorder used by Malcolm X to record his powerful speeches evokes his enduring presence and impact on the struggle for black liberation.

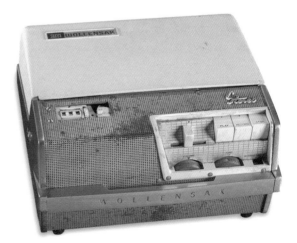

Malcolm X, revolutionary activist and minister for the Nation of Islam, used this machine to record his speeches during the early 1960s.

Emmett Till

In the summer of 1955, a fourteen-year-old boy named Emmett Till traveled from Chicago to Mississippi to visit relatives. His mother, Mamie, had worried about sending her son to the Jim Crow South, but despite her misgivings she reluctantly agreed to let him go. On August 31, Emmett's body was found floating in the Tallahatchie River. He had been abducted, beaten, and murdered by two white men in retaliation for allegedly insulting a white woman at a local grocery store. When she brought Emmett home to Chicago to be buried, Mamie Till made the courageous decision to display her son's brutalized body in an open casket in order to expose the violence and injustice inflicted on African Americans in the South. For five days, thousands of mourners filed past the glass-topped casket at Roberts Temple Church of God in Christ in Chicago to view Emmett's body, and news of his death spread around the world.

The murder of Emmett Till was a galvanizing event in the modern Civil Rights Movement. On view in a special alcove dedicated to this story is the original casket in which Emmett's body was displayed and buried in 1955. In 2005, as part of a new federal investigation into Emmett's murder (the two men accused of the crime had been acquitted by an all-white jury in 1955, though both later admitted to their guilt), the body was exhumed for an autopsy and then reburied in a new coffin. The original casket remained in storage at the cemetery until 2009, when the family granted permission for it to be donated to the museum in memory of Emmett Till and his mother, Mamie Till-Mobley.

Angola Prison Guard Tower

Near the entrance to the Emmett Till display is another artifact that recalls the history of racial violence and injustice in the South: a guard tower from Angola, the Louisiana State Penitentiary. After the Civil War, slavery was replaced by the convict-lease system, in which African Americans and poor whites were arrested and imprisoned for minor infractions so they could be leased out by the state as laborers for agriculture, industry, and public works projects. The Louisiana State Penitentiary, established in 1901 on the site of a former slave plantation known as Angola, was an example of the state-run prison farms that generated revenue through captive labor. Angola also became notorious for its abusive treatment of prisoners, who were placed under constant surveillance and subjected to whippings and other punishments. Guard towers like the one on display here symbolized the power and control that prison officials wielded over inmates' lives. To learn more about the history of Angola and the lives of African Americans who have been incarcerated there, visit *The Power of Place* exhibition in the Community Galleries on the third floor.

Interactive Lunch Counter

When four African American college students decided to stage a sit-in at a segregated Woolworth's lunch counter in Greensboro, North Carolina, in February 1960, their actions brought nationwide attention to the strategies and tactics that civil rights activists were applying across the South to dismantle the system of legal segregation. Five years later, in March 1965, a group of determined activists marched fifty miles from Selma to Montgomery, Alabama, to protest voter discrimination and demand equal protection of their rights as citizens. The march, begun with 300 people under the shadow of violence that had ended earlier attempts, ended with 25,000 people gathering in triumph on the grounds of the Alabama State Capitol.

In a large space at the center of the exhibition, an interactive lunch counter puts you into

A guard tower from Louisiana's Angola prison recalls the legacy of slavery and Jim Crow in the U.S. penal system.

the shoes—and onto the stools—of civil rights activists to understand how their individual choices and collective actions changed history. Here you can explore scenarios drawn from real events of the Civil Rights Movement, such as the Greensboro sit-in and the Selma march, and consider what choices you would have made or actions you would have taken in those situations. As you sit at the lunch counter, a panoramic video featuring news coverage of civil rights demonstrations immerses you in the events of the movement in real time.

At the interactive lunch counter, visitors explore how civil rights activists brought about social change.

Southern Railway No. 1200

On a platform adjacent to the guard tower, a segregated railroad passenger car offers visitors a firsthand encounter with the separate and unequal conditions that African Americans experienced while living and traveling under Jim Crow. During the 1940s, the Southern Railway Company operated a long-distance passenger service between Washington, D.C., and New Orleans. To comply with state laws that required public transportation to be segregated, the company outfitted this coach with a partition to create separate seating sections for white and black passengers. While both sections have the same reclining seats, the white section is twice as large and has larger restrooms as well as lounges for passenger use. Visitors can look inside the coach, now restored to its 1940s' condition, and walk alongside the full length of the car to view the segregated seating areas for black and white passengers.

Displays near the railroad car explore the history of segregated transportation and the long-fought battle by African Americans to challenge and end the practice. This area also includes a display about Pullman porters and coach attendants who worked on segregated railroad cars, helped black travelers navigate the Jim Crow landscape, and served as vital sources of information for the African American community.

The Tuskegee Airmen's Stearman Kaydet

As the nation prepared to enter World War II, African Americans serving in the segregated armed forces had to convince military officials that they had the intelligence, discipline, and skill to be combat pilots. The first group of black aviation cadets began training at Moton Field in Tuskegee, Alabama, in July 1941, and graduated in March 1942. By 1946, nearly a thousand

A segregated railroad car of the Southern Railway Company illustrates the separate—and unequal—conditions that black travelers experienced under Jim Crow.

A biplane flown by Tuskegee Airmen during combat training soars over the ramp leading up from *The Era of Segregation* landing theater.

black airmen had earned their U.S. Army Air Corps pilot wings at Tuskegee. Under the command of Lt. Col. Benjamin O. Davis Jr., the Tuskegee Airmen served with distinction in World War II, receiving more than one hundred and fifty Distinguished Flying Crosses for their heroism in the air.

Soaring above you as you leave the exhibition is a 1944 Stearman PT-13D Kaydet flown by the Tuskegee Airmen during their training at Moton Field. The two-seater biplane, originally produced by the Stearman Aircraft Company and later manufactured by Boeing, was the standard model used by the U.S. military to train pilots during the 1930s and 1940s. This Stearman was purchased in 2005 and restored by Air Force Capt. Matt Quy and his wife Tina, who christened it the *Spirit of Tuskegee* in honor of the Tuskegee Airmen. In the summer of 2011, the Quys flew the aircraft across the country from California to Washington, D.C., for its ceremonial donation to the museum.

Reflections and Landing Theater

A concluding display, "Reflections of a Generation," presents images and quotes from key individuals of the segregation era, including Martin Luther King Jr., Malcolm X, Booker T. Washington, and Ida B. Wells. An interactive recording booth invites you to share your personal stories and reflections.

At the top of the ramp leading up from the exhibition is the second of three landing theaters in the History Galleries, which presents a video highlighting the role of women in the Civil Rights Movement. This space also includes a second installment of "Journey Toward Freedom," a media interactive where you can explore stories from the History Galleries in more detail. From here you can proceed up the ramp to enter the third and final history exhibition, *A Changing America: 1968 and Beyond.*

THE FORD FOUNDATION GALLERY

A Changing America
1968 AND BEYOND

o make of the last 50 years of progress
This exhibition examines the strategies
ve used to wrestle with racial discrimination,
ion, and economic inequality since 1968
he evolving status of the African American
ust as the Civil Rights and Black Power
ursued goals of justice and equality in the
mericans must decide how to advance
to the 21ˢᵗ century.

Documenting the past and an
not about chronicling the sweep of
of a social movement, but collecting
disparate fragments that tell
not a linear story, but a catalog

NELSON GEORGE 2016

HONOR KING: END RACISM!

The Death of Martin Luther King Jr.

Revolution is not a
one-time event.

—Audre Lorde

A CHANGING AMERICA

1968 AND BEYOND

Over the past fifty years, African Americans have continued to seek racial equity and social justice. As with previous generations, this contemporary quest for freedom has been marked both by progress and paradox, breakthroughs and backlash. *A Changing America: 1968 and Beyond*, located on the top level of the History Galleries, explores social, political, and cultural changes in American society, from the death of Martin Luther King Jr. into the twenty-first century. It examines the strategies African Americans have used to wrestle with racial discrimination, cultural exclusion, and economic inequality and considers how issues of immigration, class, and gender have reshaped the definition of African American identity at the turn of the present century.

At the exhibition entrance, a dynamic multimedia presentation evokes the turbulent and revolutionary atmosphere of the late 1960s.

A CHANGING AMERICA
1968 AND BEYOND

A Changing America: 1968 and Beyond is located on level C1, the top floor of the History Galleries, and is accessed via ramps leading up from *The Era of Segregation* on level C2. The exhibition explores political and cultural changes that have shaped American society from the late 1960s into the twenty-first century.

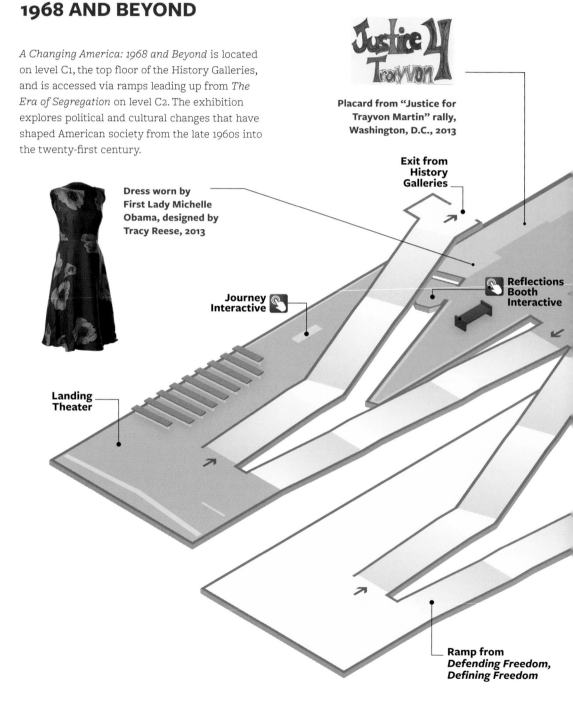

Placard from "Justice for Trayvon Martin" rally, Washington, D.C., 2013

Dress worn by First Lady Michelle Obama, designed by Tracy Reese, 2013

Exit from History Galleries

Journey Interactive

Reflections Booth Interactive

Landing Theater

Ramp from *Defending Freedom, Defining Freedom*

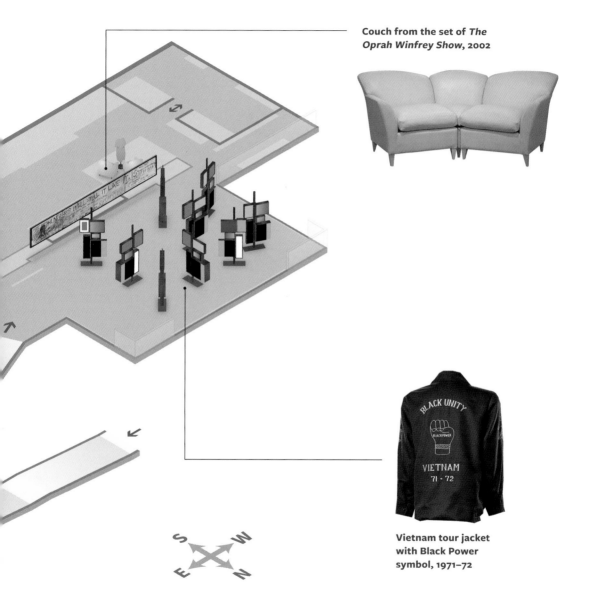

Couch from the set of *The Oprah Winfrey Show*, 2002

Vietnam tour jacket with Black Power symbol, 1971–72

The Black Power Era

The year 1968 marked a turning point in the modern struggle for African American freedom and equality. The shockwaves of grief, fury, and frustration that swept through American cities after the assassination of Martin Luther King Jr. signaled the recognition that ending Jim Crow segregation would not be enough to achieve equality and justice. Rather than seeking to convince white America to accept integration, many activists shifted their efforts to developing and strengthening black communities and promoting black pride, independence, and self-determination. As the definition of "Black Power" evolved in the late 1960s and early 1970s to represent the broader political, economic, and cultural interests of the black community, advocates also took up other issues and struggles, including women's rights, anti-colonial revolutions in African nations, and opposition to the war in Vietnam.

As you enter the exhibition, a dynamic multimedia presentation immerses you in the politics and culture of the Black Power era. Scenes and sounds from the turbulent year of 1968 play on a central overhead screen, while nine displays shaped like picket signs fan out through the space and explore the assassination of Martin Luther King Jr., religion and Black Power, the Black Panther Party, the Vietnam War, electoral politics, the Black Arts Movement, black feminism, film and television, and black middle-class consciousness. Artifacts featured in these picket displays include an anti-racism poster carried in a 1968 Martin Luther King Jr. memorial march; a uniform worn by a member of the Fruit of Islam—the security force of the Nation of Islam; a jacket with a Black Power fist logo

Women raise their fists at a Black Panther Party rally in Oakland, California, in 1968.

Shirley Chisholm was the first black woman elected to Congress and the first to run for president, in 1972.

Another section of the entrance gallery is dedicated to the Poor People's Campaign and Resurrection City, a massive live-in demonstration that occupied the National Mall for six weeks during the summer of 1968. Conceived by Martin Luther King Jr. and then led by Rev. Ralph Abernathy after King's assassination, the multiracial campaign included American Indians, Latinos, and whites. Together, they lobbied for a guaranteed minimum income, job programs, and expanded educational opportunities. A plywood mural painted with slogans from Resurrection City reflects the diversity of causes and experiences represented by the demonstrators.

worn by a black soldier in Vietnam; and buttons from Shirley Chisholm's historic campaign for president in 1972.

Along the perimeter walls of this space, large photo murals and object displays provide a wider context for the development of the Black Power Movement, tracing its roots in the modern Civil Rights Movement, the major leaders, its impact on black style and fashion, and its expressions in American popular culture. Artifacts include a 1973 record album featuring Malcolm X's famous "The Ballot or the Bullet" speech; an FBI "Wanted" poster issued for Black Panther leader Eldridge Cleaver; and an Afro pick in the form of a Black Power fist and peace sign—a symbol of African Americans embracing "natural" hairstyles and the slogan "Black is Beautiful."

The Movement Marches On

By the mid-1970s, the Black Power Movement had lost much of its momentum due to government repression, internal conflicts, a conservative backlash, and the evidence of some progress toward equality. This did not mean the end of activism, however, as African Americans continued to organize in support of equal access and opportunity and to demand racial justice. These efforts also included the promotion of African American history and culture through the founding of museums and black studies programs at colleges and universities across the United States. Moreover, the black liberation movement inspired and encouraged Latinos, Asian Americans, American Indians, women, gays, and those at the intersection of these identities to organize their own social justice movements.

"Hunger's Wall" is a mural created by antipoverty activists at the Resurrection City encampment in Washington, D.C., in 1968.

Mexican Americans also organized for civil rights and social justice under the banner of "Chicano Power." This poster dates from the 1970s.

Objects in this section illustrate the continued resonance and wider impact of the Black Power Movement, including a poster proclaiming "Chicano Power"; a button promoting the nascent gay rights movement; an anti-racist poster produced by the National Organization for Women; a banner supporting inmates who led an uprising in Attica, New York, to protest conditions at the prison; and a 1969 black studies textbook, *A People's College Primer.*

Shifting Landscapes: Cities and Suburbs

As the rise of African American political power and cultural influence continued through the 1970s, black mobility improved, afforded by better jobs and better pay. Attracted by more spacious homes and improved municipal services, black families moved, when they could,

from the inner city to the suburbs. Yet in both city and suburb, African American homeowners faced higher rates on bank loans and the prospect of declining property values when whites refused to live in integrated neighborhoods. Meanwhile, as corporations moved factories out of the cities or out of the country, they took away manufacturing jobs that had long been the mainstay of urban black families. Just as black politicians were elected to local office, city governments found it increasingly difficult to provide good housing, schools, roads, police, health care, and even garbage disposal. Activists and neighborhood organizations created programs to address the needs of urban residents and protested against policies that unfairly targeted minorities and the poor.

This section of *A Changing America* explores the opportunities and challenges of urban and suburban life for African Americans during the

Pamphlet promoting Soul City, a planned community developed in 1969 by civil rights activist Floyd McKissick.

1970s and 1980s. Featured objects include a brick façade from the Baxter Terrace public housing project in Newark, New Jersey; a booklet copy of the Fair Housing Act of 1968, prohibiting racial discrimination in the sale or rental of housing; and a pamphlet for Soul City, North Carolina, a planned community developed by civil rights activist Floyd McKissick. A narrated video in this section examines the changing demographics of black populations in the U.S. during the final decades of the twentieth century.

Decades of Paradox and Promise, 1970–2015

Given the progress made over the previous generation, African Americans entered the final quarter of the twentieth century with some cautious optimism. Affirmative action bolstered enrollment at universities, while federal and city hiring provided black families with better job options. Enterprising women and men pursued advanced degrees and gained footholds in professional sectors. The immigration of hundreds of thousands of Africans and Afro-Caribbeans changed the face of black America and contributed new perspectives on the United States as a land of freedom and opportunity.

However, as the African American community grew more culturally and politically diverse, economic gains also intensified class divisions between more affluent blacks and the urban

poor. In an era when African Americans achieved unprecedented influence in American cultural and political affairs—symbolized most profoundly by the 2008 election of Barack H. Obama as the forty-fourth president of the United States—black communities continued to face institutional racism, police violence, increased incarceration, and substandard education, housing, and health care. Other events, such as the government's failure to respond to the needs of black communities devastated by Hurricane Katrina in New Orleans and the killings of Trayvon Martin and other unarmed black men that fueled the rise of the Black Lives Matter movement, proved how far the nation still had to go at the dawn of the twenty-first century to realize the goals of racial equity and social justice.

In this section of the exhibition, a series of multimedia displays take you, decade by decade, from the 1970s through the mid-2010s. Objects, images, music, and video serve as touchstones for major political, social, and cultural events and evoke the sights and sounds of the era. Artifact highlights from each decade include an antibusing license plate depicting segregationist politician George Wallace and a poster from the popular 1975 film *Cooley High*; memorabilia from Jesse Jackson's historic 1984 presidential campaign and a boom box carried by the character Radio Raheem in Spike Lee's 1989 film *Do the Right Thing*; a button supporting Anita Hill for her testimony in the 1991 confirmation hearings for U.S. Supreme Court justice Clarence

Thomas and a sweatshirt from the 1995 Million Man March; a Florida voting booth from the hotly contested 2000 presidential election and a U.S. Coast Guard rescue basket used during Hurricane Katrina in 2005; and a placard from a protest outside the White House after the killing of black teenager Trayvon Martin in 2012.

Also in this section are three case studies that focus on significant topics, people, and events that shaped American culture and society over the past several decades. The first features a re-created stage set from *The Oprah Winfrey Show*, the influential daytime television talk show hosted and produced by Oprah Winfrey from 1986 to 2011. The second case study examines the social relevance of hip-hop music and culture, illustrated with a large Public Enemy banner used during performances by the group led by rapper and activist Chuck D. The third and final case study is devoted to the presidential campaign and election of Barack Obama, and features a display of posters and other memorabilia as well as a dress worn by First Lady Michelle Obama for the fiftieth anniversary, in 2013, of the March on Washington.

Reflections of a Generation

A Changing America concludes with a video dialogue about African American identity, featuring five contemporary activists and thinkers: Jay Smooth, commentator and hip-hop radio personality; Semhar Araia, lawyer and African diaspora consultant; Opal Tometi, community organizer and a cofounder of the Black Lives Matter movement; M. K. Asante, professor, author, and rapper; and Jeff Johnson, journalist and commentator. As in the other history exhibitions, an interactive recording booth is available for you to share your own stories and thoughts. At the top of the ramp leading out of the exhibition is a landing theater, where a final video presents a conversation on race that reflects on progress made and issues still to be resolved as Americans head further into the twenty-first century. There is also a final installment of the "Journey Toward Freedom" media interactive where you can dig deeper into stories and events explored in the exhibition.

When Hurricane Katrina struck in 2005, baskets such as this were used to rescue those caught in the flood waters. However, the slow and inadequate efforts of government officials to help stranded residents, most of them black and poor, drew widespread condemnation and charges of racism.

COMMUNITY

LIFTING
AS
WE CLIMB

> The outside world told black kids ... that we weren't worth anything. But our parents said it wasn't so, and our churches and our schoolteachers said it wasn't so. They believed in us, and we, therefore, believed in ourselves.
>
> —MARIAN WRIGHT EDELMAN

COMMUNITY GALLERIES

MAKING A WAY OUT OF NO WAY

 MAKING A WAY OUT OF NO WAY

 THE POWER OF PLACE

 DOUBLE VICTORY: THE AFRICAN AMERICAN MILITARY EXPERIENCE

 SPORTS: LEVELING THE PLAYING FIELD

A sense of community—forged by shared experiences, nurtured through organizations and institutions, and expressed through values of service, mutual assistance, and uplift—has been a core component of African American life and a key to surviving racial oppression. On the third floor of the National Museum of African American History and Culture, exhibitions explore different ways in which African Americans have created and cultivated this sense of community. As African Americans organized for mutual benefit and support, participated in sports and military service, and built places to live, learn, work, worship, and play, they also carved out spaces for pursuing political goals and effecting social change.

Bearing a motto of racial uplift, this silk banner from an Oklahoma women's organization dates from the 1920s.

COMMUNITY GALLERIES

The museum's third floor features four exhibitions that explore different ways that African Americans have cultivated a sense of community and created bases for social change: *Making a Way Out of No Way*; *The Power of Place*; *Double Victory: The African American Military Experience*; and *Sports: Leveling the Playing Field*.

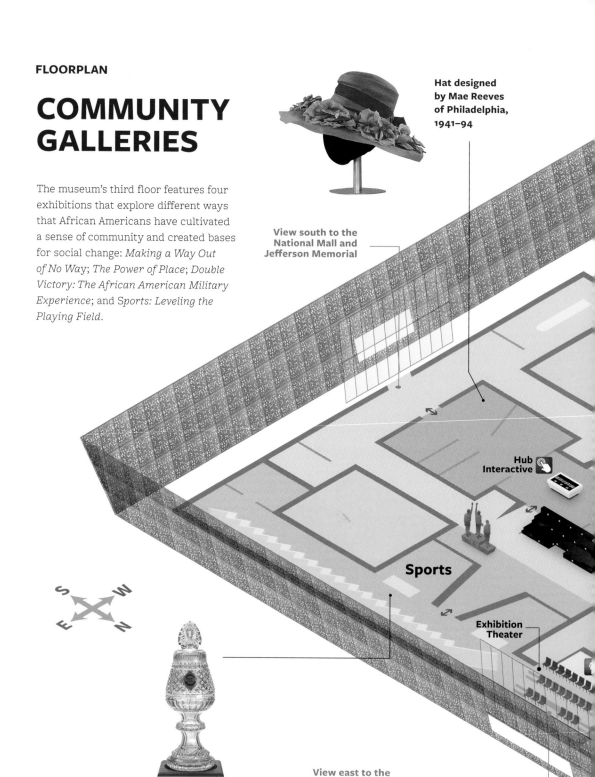

Hat designed by Mae Reeves of Philadelphia, 1941–94

View south to the National Mall and Jefferson Memorial

Hub Interactive

Sports

Exhibition Theater

Bayou Classic Trophy, 2014

View east to the National Museum of American History

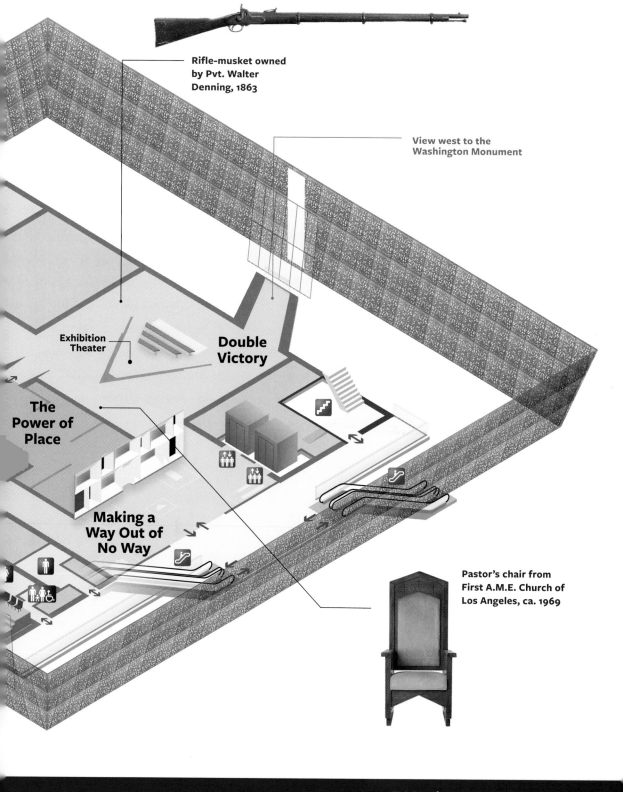

Rifle-musket owned
by Pvt. Walter
Denning, 1863

View west to the
Washington Monument

Exhibition
Theater

Double
Victory

The
Power of
Place

Making a
Way Out of
No Way

Pastor's chair from
First A.M.E. Church of
Los Angeles, ca. 1969

On the local, state, and national levels, Negro Americans gained ground through the kind of self-help that had characterized our struggle since slavery—by creating our own organizations to meet our needs.

—Dorothy Height

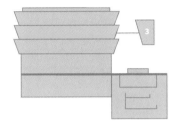

MAKING A WAY OUT OF NO WAY

Taking its title from a popular African American expression, *Making a Way Out of No Way* explores different strategies that black communities have used for survival and support and to effect social change. At the entrance, a multiscreen media wall and iconic artifacts introduce the major topics of the exhibition. The display includes desks from a Rosenwald school built to educate African American children in the Jim Crow South; a workers' time clock from the National Baptist Publishing Board, a prominent black-owned business in Nashville; and a banner from the Oklahoma Federation of Colored Women's Clubs, bearing the motto of the National Association of Colored Women, "Lifting as We Climb."

Making a Way Out of No Way continues down the halls on either side of the media wall, encircling the Community floor. Each section is organized around a central theme: Faith, Education, Organizations, Enterprise, Press, and Activism.

Through education, faith, and other community institutions, African Americans forged possibilities in a world that denied them opportunities.

Foundations of Faith

African Americans developed diverse religious institutions, from the first independent congregations established by free blacks in the early 1800s to contemporary black churches, temples, mosques, and synagogues. These institutions served as centers of moral and political leadership, promoted values of self-determination and pride, and provided services and support to urban and rural communities. Spiritual beliefs and faith practices offered hope, comfort, and the will to resist oppression.

In the Foundations of Faith section of *Making a Way Out of No Way*, evocative historical images, quotations, and artifacts illuminate the central role of faith and religious institutions in developing and sustaining black communities. The diversity of African American religious traditions is reflected in objects such as an usher badge from New Bethany Baptist Church in Washington, D.C.; a Jewish shofar used by Beth Shalom B'nai Zaken Ethiopian Hebrew Congregation in Chicago; and a Qur'an owned by African American Muslim leader Imam Warith Deen Mohammed. Other objects, including a writing slate book owned by Bishop Benjamin Tucker Tanner of the A.M.E. Church and an issue of *Soul Force*, the journal of the Southern Christian Leadership Conference, testify to the engagement of black religious leaders in issues of education and civil rights.

Several stories in this section trace the founding and development of prominent black religious institutions. First A.M.E. Church of Los Angeles was cofounded in 1872 by Bridget "Biddy" Mason, a formerly enslaved woman who successfully sued for her freedom in 1856. Working as a nurse and midwife, she invested in property and amassed a sizable fortune, which she used to establish the church and cultivate a legacy of community service. St. Augustine Catholic Church, a landmark in the Tremé neighborhood of New Orleans since it was founded in 1842, served a racially diverse congregation that reflected the various segments of New Orleans society. Among its parishioners was Homer Plessy, whose arrest for sitting in the white section of a Jim Crow railroad car resulted in the 1896 Supreme Court decision establishing the doctrine of "separate but equal."

Under the leadership of Elijah Muhammad, the Nation of Islam served as a spiritual sanctuary and self-help organization for millions of African Americans for over forty years. After Muhammad's death in 1975, his son, Warith Deen Mohammed, led many former NOI members to convert to mainstream Islam. "Muslim Americans: Claiming a National Identity" explores this story and examines the significance of the Muslim faith for African Americans. The fourth and final display in this section profiles Florence Spearing Randolph, a women's rights activist and preacher in the A.M.E. Zion Church, who was one of the first American women to become an ordained minister.

Ceremonial ram's horn, or shofar, used at Beth Shalom synagogue, a black Jewish congregation in Chicago, 1998.

(HBCUs) in providing educational opportunities and promoting academic achievement is represented by items such as a pennant from Wilberforce University, founded in Ohio in 1856 as the nation's first private university for black students; a diploma from the Colored Training School in Baltimore, today known as Coppin State University; and an industrial education award from Prairie View A&M University, the first state-supported black college in Texas. Other objects, including the 1928 textbook *Negro Makers of History* written by pioneering African American historian Carter G. Woodson, speak of efforts to change the nature of education itself and enable black students to see themselves reflected more positively and accurately in the subjects they learned in school.

A schoolroom setting, complete with desks, a wood-burning stove, and a wooden sign from the Hope School in Pomaria, South Carolina, tells the story of a remarkable effort to address the lack of equal educational opportunities for black children in the segregated rural South. The Rosenwald schools program, created by white philanthropist Julius Rosenwald and black educator Booker T. Washington, helped to fund the construction of over 5,300 schools in fifteen states between 1917 and 1932. In addition to learning about the history of the Hope School, a Rosenwald school that operated from 1925 to 1954, you can also see video

Pastor's chair from First A.M.E. Church of Los Angeles, ca. 1969.

The Value of Education

Whether enslaved or free, of limited means or from a privileged background, African Americans—like so many Americans—viewed education as the key to changing their status. Communities banded together to build and support schools, and parents sacrificed to send their children far from home. Despite various obstacles, African Americans sought education— from the basics to higher intellectual pursuits— that established a lasting legacy of achievement.

Artifacts displayed in this section of *Making a Way Out of No Way* signify the value that black communities have invested in education. The vital role of historically black colleges and universities

Industrial Education Award from Prairie View A&M University, Texas, ca. 1960.

EDUCATION

THE HOPE SCHOOL

African Americans managed to obtain education for their children by pooling their own resources with philanthropic support. This two-room school in Pomaria, South Carolina, was one of thousands of schools built in the rural South with aid [from the Ju]lius Rosenwald Fund. The Hope School [operated until Ap]ril 1954 when it closed as a result [of school con]solidation efforts. In

SEGREGATED EDUCATION

ROSENWALD SCHOOLS

Student nurse's uniform worn by Pauline Brown Payne, Homer G. Phillips Hospital, St. Louis, 1944.

white-run medical schools and hospitals were closed to aspiring black nurses and physicians, separate black institutions like Homer G. Phillips Hospital in St. Louis, Missouri, provided access to professional training as well as improved health care for local black communities.

The topic of segregated education is explored from another perspective in a story about the township of Covert, Michigan, where public schools—and the community as a whole—operated on a racially integrated basis from the 1850s onward. This section also includes a display about Ben Carson, the neurosurgeon, philanthropist, and politician who has used his personal story of overcoming urban poverty through education to inspire children to maximize their intellectual potential.

interviews with former students describing their experiences attending the Hope School.

Several stories in the Value of Education section touch on themes of science and medicine, which have been critical to the African American educational experience. W. Montague Cobb, the first African American to earn a doctorate in physical anthropology, established a world-class anatomical laboratory at Howard University in the 1930s, which he used to conduct groundbreaking research that challenged conventional notions of black racial inferiority. During the segregation era, when most

The Hope School in Pomaria, South Carolina, was one of thousands of Rosenwald schools built to educate black children during the segregation era.

Organizing for Success

For centuries, African Americans have formed associations for mutual benefit and advancement. While many black organizations emerged in response to segregation, they also promoted cultural values of community, education, and service. Membership provided opportunities to develop leadership skills, pool resources, and cultivate a sense of pride and belonging. As African Americans organized for success, they created ways to help themselves and built powerful networks that could be mobilized to work for social change.

In this section of *Making a Way Out of No Way*, objects and archival images reflect the membership and activities of various African American organizations. A booklet from the Brotherhood of Sleeping Car Porters, organized by A. Philip Randolph in 1925 to improve conditions for black employees of the Pullman railroad company, and a seal from Sigma Pi Phi, a fraternity for black professional men founded in Philadelphia in 1904, symbolize efforts to promote economic opportunity and social advancement. The leadership and achievements of African

American women are represented by a bronze award statuette and membership pin from The Links, Inc., a volunteer service organization founded in 1946 to promote African American cultural and economic development; and an elaborate ceremonial collar worn by an officer of the Daughters of Elks, the women's auxiliary to the Improved Benevolent and Protective Order of Elks of the World (IBPOEW). Through membership in fraternal organizations such as the Elks, black men and women cultivated leadership, self-respect, and solidarity.

Stories in this section reveal that while some African American fraternal organizations were based on traditionally white organizations, they served unique cultural and social functions within the black community. The Prince Hall Masons, an African American Masonic order founded in Boston and chartered by the Grand Lodge of England in 1784, practiced the rituals and doctrines of Freemasonry while also promoting ideals of mutual aid, racial uplift, and black male identity. First established in the early twentieth century, Black Greek-letter Organizations served as support networks for black students at traditionally white schools and the center of campus social life at historically black colleges and universities. The oldest and largest black fraternities and sororities, known

Master Mason's apron from the Prince Hall Grand Lodge of Massachusetts, late 1700s.

as the Divine Nine, have fostered traditions of leadership and community service among their members, who include many prominent figures in business, politics, science, sports, and entertainment. A third story in this section examines the Independent Order of St. Luke (IOSL), an organization dedicated to promoting economic self-help for African Americans during the segregation era. Led by Maggie Lena Walker from 1899 to 1934, the IOSL had more than 100,000 members at its peak, with business operations that included a bank, an insurance company, a department store, and a newspaper. Today, Walker's home in Richmond, Virginia, is preserved by the National Park Service as the Maggie L. Walker National Historic Site.

An Enterprising Spirit

In pursuing the American dream of economic opportunity, African Americans also created institutions to empower black communities. Skilled artisans, inventors, and entrepreneurs who achieved financial success invested their wealth to help open doors for others. Black-owned businesses provided goods and services as well as employment and places for social interaction. As African Americans integrated the workforce and the marketplace, their efforts helped to promote equal opportunities for all.

Member badge for Alpha Kappa Alpha, the first Greek-letter sorority for black women, founded in 1908.

Objects and images displayed in this section evoke the African American spirit of enterprise as expressed through labor, business, and innovation. A group of slave badges issued by the city of Charleston, South Carolina, in the early 1800s represents the skills of enslaved workers and artisans who were hired out by slaveholders; in some cases, men and women were able to buy their way out of slavery with money earned by their hired labor. Prominent black entrepreneurs are represented by artifacts such as a silver beverage service from Wormley's Hotel in Washington, D.C. James Wormley, a free black man, trained as a steward and a caterer before opening his own hotel in 1871; located across the street from the White House, Wormley's served an elite clientele, including members of Congress.

A sign for Madam C. J. Walker beauty products represents another famous entrepreneur; Walker, born Sarah Breedlove, established a lucrative system of beauty schools and sales agents to promote her hair-care products for African American consumers. Other items—a sign from the Nation of Islam's International Trades Division and a business card from one of Pepsi-Cola's first black salesmen—speak to historical debates about whether the black community would be best served by establishing its economic independence or by integrating white-owned industries.

Workers' time clock used at the National Baptist Publishing Board plant, Nashville, ca. 1912.

The work of black inventors is highlighted here through two case studies. Garrett Morgan patented several devices, including a traffic signal and a gas mask, and also developed hair-straightening products. A prototype of Morgan's gas mask, which he invented in 1912 and marketed as the National Safety Hood, is on display here. Henry Boyd, a formerly enslaved carpenter and master mechanic, became a successful furniture manufacturer in Cincinnati in the 1840s and 1850s. On view is one of Boyd's famous wooden bedsteads, which he advertised as "warranted superior to any other ever offered in the West; they can be put up or taken apart in one fourth of the time usually required, are more firm, less apt to become loose and worthless, and without a single harbor for vermin."

Stories about black-owned businesses include the National Baptist Publishing Board, founded by R. H. Boyd in 1896, which supplied publications and other materials for black churches and also served as a hub for black business development in Nashville. Known today as the R. H. Boyd Publishing Corporation, it is one of the oldest continuously operated, family-run African American businesses. The Pacific Parachute Company, one of the first black-owned World

Silver sugar bowl from Wormley's Hotel, Washington, D.C., ca. 1885.

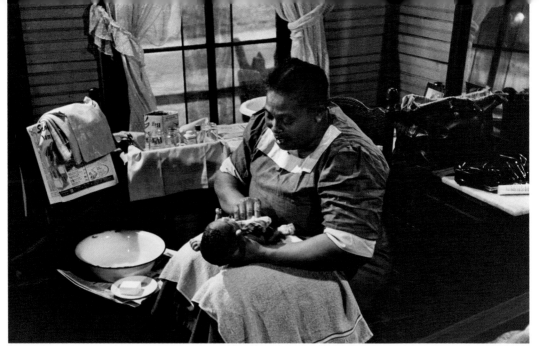

Mary Coley, a midwife in Albany, Georgia, in a scene from the 1952 educational film *All My Babies*.

War II production plants, was founded in San Diego in 1942 by aviator and businessman Howard "Skippy" Smith. The U.S. government promoted the company as an example of "democracy in action" due to its racially integrated workforce.

The Enterprising Spirit section also explores traditional occupations that have served and supported African American communities. "Making a Way on the Bay" looks at the role of black watermen in the Chesapeake Bay seafood industry and features equipment used by Ira Wright, an oysterman who lived on Maryland's Eastern Shore. You can also hear the voice of Ira Wright's son, Frank Wright, talking about his father's work on the water. A story about African American midwives examines how women practiced the midwifery profession in rural communities from the 1920s through the 1980s.

The Power of the Press

The first African American newspaper, *Freedom's Journal*, was published in 1827. Ever since, African Americans have used the press to establish an independent voice for black communities and advance the struggle for freedom and equality. Publishers and journalists challenged racism by exposing injustice, reporting on civil rights activism, and presenting positive images of black identity and achievement. Publications also reflected the diversity of black people in the United States and throughout the diaspora.

Objects and images in this section reflect different expressions of the power of the black press, across place and time. An 1842

The nation's oldest continuously published black newspaper, *The Philadelphia Tribune*, was founded by Christopher J. Perry in 1884.

edition of the *Anti-Slavery Almanac* recalls the use of the press in advancing the cause of the abolitionist movement, while a 1960 publication from the American Society of African Culture, *The American Negro Writer and His Roots*, documents the development of diaspora studies among black intellectuals during the twentieth century. A sign from *The Philadelphia Tribune* and printing blocks from the *Chicago Defender* represent two of the most prominent titles out of hundreds of black newspapers launched between 1865 and 1910.

Several stories in this section feature African Americans who worked in the newspaper business as publishers, journalists, and photographers. Mary Ann Shadd Cary, the first African American woman to publish and edit a newspaper, launched the *Provincial Freeman* after emigrating to Canada in the early 1850s. She used the paper as a platform for her views on abolition, women's rights, and black emigration. Charles "Teenie" Harris worked as a staff photographer for *The Pittsburgh Courier*, one of the nation's most prominent black newspapers during the era of segregation. Harris's photographs, spanning the 1940s to the 1970s, captured a rich documentary record of everyday life in Pittsburgh's African American community. Robert Churchwell, known as the "Jackie Robinson of Journalism," became one of the first black reporters to work at a white-owned newspaper in the segregated South, when the *Nashville Banner* hired him in 1950.

One of the oldest and most successful black-owned publications, *Ebony* magazine, was founded by John H. Johnson in 1945 to showcase images of African American achievement, glamour, and success. *Ebony* was also the first magazine to publish national-brand advertisements featuring black models. Broadside Press, an independent literary press founded by Dudley Randall in Detroit in 1965, was a leading publisher of poetry of the Black Arts movement during the late 1960s and early 1970s. Here you can read a sampling of poetry

Typewriter used by Nashville newspaper journalist Robert Churchwell, 1970s.

broadsides, representing the work of poets such as Gwendolyn Brooks, Langston Hughes, and Amiri Baraka, and also listen to a poetry reading by Haki Madhubuti, formerly known as Don L. Lee, who recorded an album released by Broadside Press in 1970.

A Tradition of Activism

Throughout history, African Americans have taken action to improve their lives and challenge the nation to live up to its democratic ideals. Working both within and across racial lines, black activists mobilized to abolish slavery, secure civil rights, fight poverty and injustice, and expand social and economic opportunities. They employed strategies ranging from legal battles to mass protests, grassroots campaigns, and public debate. By believing that change was possible, they empowered themselves to change history.

In the Tradition of Activism section, stories illuminate different forms that African American activism has taken over the past century through objects, archival images, and audio and video clips of activists speaking in their own words. A story about the Niagara Movement, the civil rights group founded by W. E. B. Du Bois and William Monroe Trotter in 1905, features an interview with Du Bois recounting an event that inspired his transformation from academic to activist. When Du Bois was a professor at Atlanta University in 1899, he was walking downtown one day and saw the fingers and toes of a man who had been lynched on display in a meat market. That moment made him realize, in his words, that "Knowledge wasn't enough"— that he had to find a way to motivate people to take direct and immediate action against racism.

This section also examines the "Don't Buy Where You Can't Work" campaigns of the 1930s and 1940s, which demonstrated the effectiveness of direct-action tactics such as boycotting and picketing. "Students on Strike" presents the story of a group of students in Farmville, Virginia, who went on strike in 1951 to protest against poor conditions at their segregated high school and ended up going to court with the NAACP to fight for desegregation of the public schools. Their legal battle became one of five cases that resulted in the 1954 *Brown v. Board of Education* decision, which ruled that separate educational facilities for black and white students were inherently unequal. "Citizenship Schools" documents the grassroots campaign to provide literacy and citizenship training to African Americans in the South as part of voter registration efforts during the late 1950s and 1960s. The writer James Baldwin and the politician Shirley Chisholm are highlighted as individuals who embodied different ideas of what an activist could be and what forms activism could take.

At the center of this wall of activism stories, a window provides a breathtaking view out onto the National Mall. As you gaze at this historic landscape, you can also look to either side of

the window to see images and film footage of momentous events that have taken place here, from Marian Anderson's concert at the Lincoln Memorial and the March on Washington to the National Black Family Reunion and the Million Man March.

Small galleries located at both ends of the wall are dedicated to two prominent activists who made a major impact both in their own time and on future generations. A gallery

A powerful quote from Muhammad Ali and historical images of demonstrators evoke the tradition of African American activism.

devoted to Muhammad Ali traces his personal transformation from a heavyweight boxing champion to an international activist and political icon. A case shared with the *Sports* exhibition displays objects from the 5th St. Gym in Miami where Ali trained during the 1960s. The other gallery features Mary McLeod Bethune, who founded the National Council of Negro Women (NCNW) in 1935 to empower African American women to become politically active and engaged on a national level.

The space is designed to evoke the Council House, the former NCNW headquarters in Washington, D.C., which is today a National Historic Site operated by the National Park Service. Here you can listen to a recording of Bethune's acclaimed "What Does American Democracy Mean to Me?" speech of 1939, browse reproductions of NCNW publications from various decades, and take a seat at an interactive conference table to exchange ideas about issues that matter most to you, your family, and your community.

The ache for home lives in all of us, the safe place where we can go as we are and not be questioned.

—RALPH ELLISON

Place Yourself

RICE FIELDS
SOUTH CAROLINA

GENEROUSLY SUPPORTED BY
LOUIS BACON/MOORE CHARITABLE FOUNDATION

It is not geography alone which determines the quality of life and culture. These depend upon the courage and personal culture of the individuals who make their home in any given locality.

—Ralph Ellison

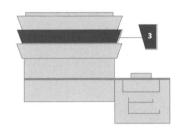

THE POWER OF PLACE

A sense of place has deeply shaped African American history and culture. A multifaceted range of African American communities and identities have formed and changed in all corners of the country and in turn influenced the regions around them. Their evolution reveals a set of stories as varied as the landscape itself.

In *The Power of Place*, you can explore stories of place from across the wide expanse of the nation and the African American experience. Your journey begins at the "Hometown Hub," an interactive media experience that presents key themes and personal stories of place. Featured places include Lyles Station, a farming community in Indiana; Oak Bluffs, a resort on Martha's Vineyard; Louisiana's Angola prison; the Bronx, New York; and Mae Reeves's hat shop in Philadelphia. Together, these cultural landscapes reflect the resiliency of African Americans in making places for themselves and overcoming the challenges they faced.

At the "Hometown Hub," personal stories shared through an interactive table reveal connections between place and memory, community, and identity.

Family, Farms, and Land in Lyles Station, Indiana

This small community near the southern border of Indiana, forty miles north of the Ohio River, offers a window into the largely unknown story of free black pioneers on the American frontier. African American farmers have been cultivating their own land in and near what became known as Lyles Station since 1815. Through changing times and cycles of prosperity and hardship, the community of Lyles Station has rested on the pillars of home, farm, church, and school—and on an unbroken history of land ownership.

Images and artifacts in this section illuminate the rural ways of life, family traditions, and deep connections to the land among the settlers of Lyles Station. Highlights include a plow used by Joshua Lyles, whose family migrated to Indiana from Tennessee in the 1830s; and a "pineapple" quilt presented as a wedding gift to Lucy Hardiman Roundtree in 1885. The display also features a jar of soil collected in 2016 from one of the earliest plots farmed by the Greer family, who have continuously cultivated their own land in Lyles Station since 1854.

Family heirlooms and photographs tell the story of Lyles Station, Indiana, an African American farming community established in the early 1800s.

3

Black Routes West

Generations before slave traders brought Africans to Jamestown, people of African descent arrived in the American West. In the 1520s, an enslaved man named Esteban de Dorantes survived a failed Spanish expedition to Florida and ultimately trekked across present-day Texas and the Southwest. Over the centuries many others followed, their histories intersecting with those of Anglos, Latinos, and American Indians, their stories and lives enriching and complicating current understanding of the wide region.

In this section, a large video presentation provides a glance into the explorations, settlements, and long history of African Americans in the American West. Personal experiences of the racial frontier are represented by objects from six different stories across the region, including the service revolver and journal of Richard Jones, who accompanied General Philip Sheridan on an expedition to Yellowstone in 1882; and silverware carried by Lavinia Whiteside, an enslaved girl, on her journey from South Carolina to Texas in the early 1860s. Other object highlights include a stitching pony used by William Sugg, a harness maker and teamster in Sonora, California, during the Gold Rush; and a cattle-branding iron owned by Calvin Bell, a cowboy who settled in southeastern Texas after the Civil War.

Camera from the photo studio of H. C. Anderson, Greenville, Mississippi, 1960s.

H. C. Anderson's Greenville, Mississippi

From the late 1940s through the 1970s, photographer Henry Clay Anderson recorded an insider's picture of black life in the city of Greenville, Mississippi, during and after the era of segregation. Born in 1911, Anderson spent most of his life in the Mississippi Delta, where he also served the community as a minister, a Mason, and a voting rights activist. Seen through Anderson's lens, Greenville is a place of spirit and resolve—a community where the black middle class refused to be defined and held captive by the systemic injustice and racial stereotypes of the time.

The photographs on the surrounding walls represent a sampling of thousands of images taken by H. C. Anderson over the years. Together they reflect a spectrum of black life in Greenville, from joyful weddings and high-school graduations to tragedies such as the funeral of assassinated NAACP leader George W. Lee. Accompanying the images are cameras and other equipment used by Anderson in his studio, along with personal effects, including his Bible, Masonic apron, and membership card from a local voting rights organization. You can also use a map and flipbook to explore the work of other black photography studios across the United States.

Calvin Bell, a rancher in southeast Texas, designed this U-shaped cattle brand in honor of his wife, Unistine, ca. 1878.

Riot and Resilience in Tulsa, Oklahoma

In late May 1921, clashes between black and white residents of Tulsa, Oklahoma, spiraled into the deadliest in a series of race riots that convulsed the United States in the early twentieth century. White mobs rampaged through the thriving black community of Greenwood, looting and burning homes, churches, and businesses and murdering scores of African Americans. Nearly a century after the riot, the people of Tulsa continue to struggle to understand and repair this event's legacy.

Tulsa's story of violence, destruction, and survival is preserved through fragments—small objects, images, and testimonies—that illuminate the lives of people who suffered tragic loss and strove for resolution and repair. Graphic postcards and charred pennies retrieved from the rubble capture the grim aftermath of the riots. A desk from the Dreamland Theatre, destroyed in the riots and later rebuilt, tells the story of the Williams family, who owned several businesses in the Greenwood commercial district known as "Black Wall Street." A video presents testimonies from survivors of the Tulsa race riot and others who have helped to lead the movement for justice and reconciliation.

After the 1921 Tulsa riot, five-year-old George Monroe found these charred pennies and kept them as souvenirs.

Leisure Culture in Oak Bluffs, Martha's Vineyard, Massachusetts

Just south of Cape Cod, on the island of Martha's Vineyard, is Oak Bluffs, a popular vacation destination for African Americans since the late 1800s. Seeking refuge from the daily trials and affronts of racial discrimination, African American families fashioned Oak Bluffs into a place of their own—a community of culture, affluence, and leisure. With its tranquil beaches, ornate cottages, lavish porch parties, and thriving businesses, Oak Bluffs remains the heart of the African American community on the Vineyard.

Artifacts and images in this section reflect the experiences of those who have lived, worked, and summered in Oak Bluffs over the past century. They include a sign, guestbook, and wicker porch furniture from Shearer Cottage, the oldest African

Oak Bluffs, a seaside community on Martha's Vineyard, has served as both vacation destination and refuge from discrimination.

American family-owned guesthouse on Martha's Vineyard, built by Charles and Henrietta Shearer in 1912. The Shearers hosted many notable guests, including politician Adam Clayton Powell Jr., who purchased his own vacation house in Oak Bluffs in 1937. Among the mementoes on display from the Powell cottage are fishing rods, beach hats, and decorative wooden "bunnies" that gave the house its nickname, "Bunny Cottage."

Oak Bluffs was just one of many vacation communities created by African Americans during the era of segregation. Illustrated flipbooks in this section provide information about other leisure destinations across the country that catered to black travelers, such as: Eureka Villa in Santa Clarita Valley, California, a 1,000-acre resort known as the "Black Palm Springs"; Idlewild, Michigan, an African American vacation community founded in 1912; and Rock Rest, a resort operated by Clayton and Hazel Sinclair in Kittery, Maine, from the 1940s through the 1970s.

Rice Fields in the Lowcountry, South Carolina

Enslaved Africans and African Americans cultivated rice along the southeastern seaboard of the United States for nearly two hundred years. The transformation of the landscape along this coast is a story of great creativity and cruel coercion, in which the culture, knowledge, and skills that enslaved people brought with them from Africa played formative roles. The reverberations of this history continue to shape the region's character.

Cultivating rice is a long and arduous process that involves tilling land, sowing, maintaining and harvesting crops, and pounding, winnowing, and milling rice grain. On display you can see an array of rice cultivation tools used by African Americans in the Lowcountry region of South Carolina, including a seed shovel, a rice pounder, and a fanner basket. Similar tools and methods have been used to cultivate rice in West Africa for hundreds of years. Accompanying the display of these implements is an evocative media piece reflecting on the history of this American landscape—a place created by the brutal pursuit of profit, a story of enslavement and exploitation as well as resilience and strength.

Mortar and pestle, a traditional tool for pounding grains of rice to strip away the hulls.

Angola, the Louisiana State Penitentiary

Built on the former site of a notorious slave plantation known as Angola, the Louisiana State Penitentiary is among the largest prisons in the United States. More than six thousand people are incarcerated there, in a compound roughly the size of Manhattan, tucked within a bend in the Mississippi River. Most of the inmates are African Americans serving life sentences. A working prison farm, Angola is a legacy of the convict-lease system that replaced slavery in the South after the Civil War, under which African Americans and poor whites were arrested and imprisoned so they could be leased out by the state to perform agricultural, industrial, and other hard labor. For most of its history, Angola has also been known as one of the nation's harshest and most inhumane prisons, although there have been significant reforms in recent decades.

An actual jail cell from the prison evokes living conditions for inmates at Angola. Measuring about 7 feet square, it is furnished with a metal sink, toilet, and bunk bed. The cell, which dates from a 1972 renovation, comes from a section of the penitentiary known as Camp A, which was originally housed in former slave quarters and later contained a disciplinary cellblock referred to as "the dungeons." Displays illustrate how those incarcerated at Angola have created and maintained a sense of community despite such conditions, including publishing a magazine, *The Angolite*, and running a hospice program for fellow inmates.

A guard tower from Angola is on exhibit in the History Galleries, as part of the exhibition *Defending Freedom, Defining Freedom: The Era of Segregation 1877–1968*.

The *Chicago Defender:* Making a Black Metropolis

During the first half of the twentieth century, the *Chicago Defender* was the largest black-owned newspaper in the nation. As an engine of ideas and opinions that galvanized black people nationwide, the newspaper spurred, shaped, and gave voice to the Great Migration of black southerners to the urban North. It also created a sense of place and an important focus for Chicago life, culture, and politics as the city changed over time.

Founded by Robert Sengstacke Abbott in 1905, the *Defender* gradually grew from a weekly publication with a local circulation of less than 300 into a daily newspaper with a national circulation of over 500,000. On display here is a linotype machine that staff used to set type for the newspaper, along with zinc plates used to print photographs. Maps and images in this section illuminate the history of Bronzeville, the African American community on Chicago's South Side that served as the newspaper's home base for many decades, while an interactive display explores issues of housing discrimination in Chicago and around the country—a major topic covered by the *Defender*.

Hip-Hop Park Jam in the Bronx, New York

Long a multiethnic, multiracial neighborhood, the Bronx experienced all the challenges that assailed New York City in the 1970s—deindustrialization and rising unemployment, crumbling infrastructure, poverty, crime, and neglect. Yet this seemingly unpromising environment became the seedbed for a vibrant new musical culture— one that would quickly grow into one of the most influential cultural forms in the world. The young people of the Bronx dubbed it Hip-Hop.

In this section, the youthful energy and innovative spirit of hip-hop are embodied in objects such as a set of turntables, speakers, and amps used by The Original DJ Tony Tone (Angelo T. King). As a teenager living in a public housing project in the Bronx, King came together with other young artists in 1978 to form the legendary group known as the Cold Crush Brothers. Images and video capture the sights and sounds of the city during this period, while maps show the locations of parks, clubs, and community centers throughout the Bronx where hip-hop music and culture took root and flourished.

By creating spaces for diverse youth cultures and musical styles to mix, exchange, and innovate, the Bronx became the birthplace of hip-hop.

CROWNING ACHIEVEMENTS:

Mae Reeves

Every woman should have at least one special hat they can put on, strut out the door, and say, "Here I am world. I feel good and I know I look good." —MAE REEVES

Photograph of Mae Reeves wearing a fox fur stole and stylish hat, 1950.

One of the ten place studies in *The Power of Place* exhibition focuses on Mae Reeves, a hat designer and entrepreneur who ran a millinery shop in Philadelphia for more than fifty years.

Born in 1912 in Vidalia, Georgia, Reeves worked as a teacher and journalist before starting her career as a milliner. She trained at the Chicago School of Millinery from 1930 to 1934, then moved to Philadelphia, where she honed her business skills selling cosmetics and working in a women's apparel shop. In 1940, she secured a $500 loan from a local black-owned bank and opened her own shop on South Street. Several years later she moved her business to West Philadelphia, and in 1953 she purchased a commercial building on 60th Street, becoming the first African American woman to own a business in that district. With creativity and business acumen, Reeves established herself as a one-of-a-kind ladies' hat maker, who attracted customers from all walks of life. "Mae of Philadelphia," as she became known, was also a community builder. She participated in church, business, and neighborhood organizations, was active in local politics, and served as a mentor to young women entrepreneurs.

The museum's collection, donated by Reeves and her children, Donna Limerick and William Mincey Jr., includes more than seventy vintage hats as well as furnishings, fabric samples, tools, and accessories from Mae's Millinery Shop that were preserved just as Reeves left them when she finally retired in 1997, at the age of eighty-five. Approximately twenty hats made by Reeves are on view in *The Power of Place* exhibition, including some of her most elaborate designs, which she called her "showstoppers." Representing half a century of women's fashion, these crowning achievements also symbolize the creativity, style, community spirit, and business acumen of the woman who fashioned them.

Above and opposite page: Hats designed by Mae Reeves, mid-1900s.

Dear wife, I have enlisted in the army ...
and though great is the difficulty yet I look
forward to a brighter day when I shall have
the opportunity of seeing you in the full
enjoyment of freedom.

—Pvt. Samuel Cabble, 1863

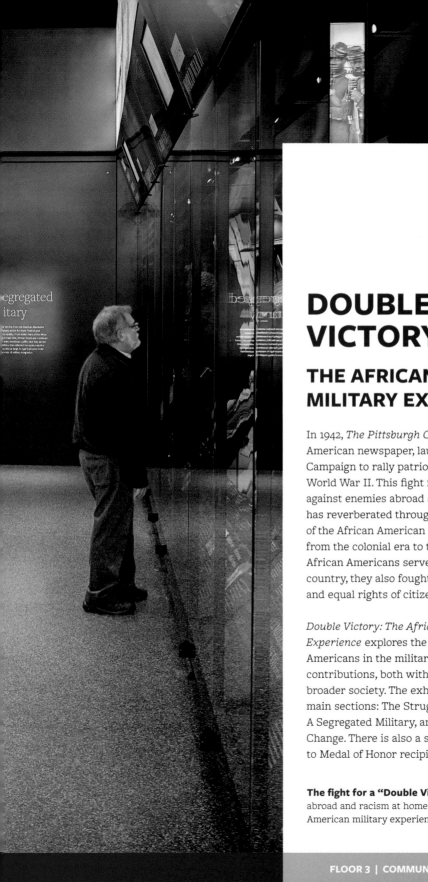

DOUBLE VICTORY

THE AFRICAN AMERICAN MILITARY EXPERIENCE

In 1942, *The Pittsburgh Courier*, an African American newspaper, launched the Double Victory Campaign to rally patriotic support during World War II. This fight for a "Double Victory"—against enemies abroad and racism at home—has reverberated throughout the long history of the African American military experience, from the colonial era to the War on Terror. As African Americans served and sacrificed for their country, they also fought to secure liberty, justice, and equal rights of citizenship.

Double Victory: The African American Military Experience explores the history of African Americans in the military and the impact of their contributions, both within the military and in the broader society. The exhibition unfolds in three main sections: The Struggle for Freedom, A Segregated Military, and The Stirrings of Change. There is also a special gallery devoted to Medal of Honor recipients.

The fight for a "Double Victory"—against enemies abroad and racism at home—has defined the African American military experience.

Ambrotype of Sgt. Qualls Tibbs, 27th U.S. Colored Troops, 1864–65.

The Struggle for Freedom

Throughout the early history of the United States, African Americans participated in conflicts that shaped the course of the nation, from the American Revolution and the War of 1812 to the Seminole Wars, the Mexican-American War, and the Civil War. Ultimately, these men and women helped to guarantee a freedom for this nation that was often denied to them.

During the Revolutionary War, thousands of African Americans served as soldiers in the American colonial armies, including Jack Little, whose 1782 pay certificate for his service in the 4th Connecticut is on display here. Even more black colonists fought for Britain, which promised freedom in return for military service. When the war ended, this promise was honored for some enslaved African Americans who had fought for the British cause, including 3,000 black loyalists who were transported to Nova Scotia. But most experienced the same fate as many African Americans who had supported

the fight for American independence: a return to slavery. The War of 1812, sometimes referred to as the Second War of Independence, opened the ranks of the U.S. Navy to skilled African American seamen. An 1826 seaman's certificate carried by Robert Barnaby is a reminder that African American sailors who fought for their country also faced the risk of being seized as slaves, especially in southern ports.

The Civil War was one of the most pivotal events in American history, and the Union victory that established the possibility of freedom for all depended on the service and sacrifice of tens of thousands of black soldiers, many formerly enslaved. Among the objects that document this service are identification tags worn by enlisted men, including Sgt. Qualls Tibbs of Orange County, Virginia. Also on view is an Army of the James Medal, commissioned by Union Gen. Benjamin Butler to honor the bravery of U.S. Colored Troops at the Battle of Chapin's Farm (also known as Chaffin's Farm or New Market Heights) in September 1864, and a musket carried by Pvt. Walter Denning of the 26th Regiment, U.S. Colored Infantry, a New York unit that was stationed in South Carolina.

A Segregated Military

From the Indian Wars of the 1860s to the start of the Korean War, African Americans continued to fight bravely in every conflict involving the United States. But they served in a segregated military that reflected the racial prejudice and exclusion of society at large.

After the Civil War, thousands of troops were garrisoned across the West to push back American Indians and open lands for settlement. African American troops who served in the West earned the nickname "Buffalo Soldiers"—for their dark curly hair, the buffalo skin coats they wore, and their bravery in battle. The soldiers gradually accepted the term as a compliment. But the irony of black men fighting red men for white men was not lost on these troops. The Buffalo Soldiers' story is told here through a display of artifacts, including a uniform worn by 2nd Lt. John Hanks Alexander, a West Point graduate who served in the 9th Cavalry, and a saddle used by a soldier in B Troop, 9th Cavalry.

When the United States entered World War I in 1917, African Americans saw a chance to once again prove their patriotism and earn an equal place in society. More than 200,000 African Americans served overseas during the war. Most worked in Services of Supply units, delivering food, weapons, equipment, and other materials to soldiers on the front lines. Of those assigned to combat duty, many served under French military command, in part because some white American officers refused to lead black troops into battle. Among the objects on display in this section are a gas mask used by the 369th Infantry Regiment, known as the Harlem Hellfighters, who received the French Croix de Guerre for their bravery in combat, and a pair of binoculars used by Lt. Peter L. Robinson, who graduated from Fort Des Moines, Iowa, the first training camp for black officers, and served in France with the 368th Infantry.

French Croix de Guerre medal awarded to Cpl. Lawrence McVey, 369th Infantry Regiment, 1918.

U.S. Army officer's dress coat worn by 2nd Lt. John Hanks Alexander, 9th Cavalry Regiment, ca. 1890.

A patriotic "Double V" handkerchief (1942–45) symbolizes the battle against racial discrimination on the home front during World War II.

While African Americans continued to serve in segregated military units during World War II, they expanded their service into all branches of the armed forces by 1943. The first African American combat pilots, the famous Tuskegee Airmen, trained for Army Air Corps service at Moton Field in Tuskegee, Alabama; among them was Woodrow R. Crockett, whose leather flight jacket and scarf are on display here. (A plane flown by the Tuskegee Airmen during their military training is on view in the History Galleries.) On the home front, activists secured a victory over racial discrimination in the defense industry and set the stage for further progress with the Double Victory Campaign.

Stirrings of Change

Victory during World War II brought African Americans one step closer to equality and civil rights. Executive Order 9981, issued in 1948, directed that "there shall be equality of treatment and opportunity for all persons in the armed services without regard to race, color, religion, or national origin." Over the next several decades, African Americans continued to serve in the armed forces in Korea and Vietnam against a backdrop of the Civil Rights Movement, the Black Power Movement, and racial tensions in the military.

The Korean War was both a battleground against communism and a proving ground for the U.S. military as it evolved into an integrated force. A drill instructor's hat on display was worn by Marine Command Sgt. Maj. Edgar R. Huff, who was among the first to integrate a combat unit in Korea. A decade later, while many African Americans joined with other Americans in opposing the Vietnam War, some found opportunities in military service and rose to leadership positions. Lloyd "Fig" Newton was commissioned a second lieutenant in the Air Force after graduating from Tennessee State University in 1966 and flew 269 combat missions during the Vietnam War. In 1974, he became the first African American pilot in the Air Force's elite demonstration team, the Thunderbirds, and retired in 2000 as a four-star general. Newton's Thunderbird Flight Demonstration Team helmet is on view here, along with the NASA flight jacket worn by Maj. Gen. Charles F. Bolden Jr., a Marine Corps aviator who went on to become an astronaut and the first black Administrator of NASA.

Since 1973, African Americans have willingly joined in the all-volunteer force and most recently are helping to defend the United States against international terrorism. Other modern military artifacts on display include the four-star U.S. Army green service uniform (also known as the Class A uniform) worn by Gen. Colin Powell, Chairman of the Joint Chiefs of Staff during the Persian Gulf War and the first African American Secretary of State. The advancement of African American women to military leadership positions is represented by a uniform worn by Hazel Johnson-Brown, who became the first African American woman general in 1979 when she was appointed Chief of the U.S. Army Nurse Corps, and a uniform worn by naval officer Michelle Howard, who in 2014 became the first woman to earn the rank of four-star admiral.

Women's U.S. Army service hat worn by Brig. Gen. Hazel Johnson-Brown, 1980.

NASA flight jacket worn by Maj. Gen. Charles F. Bolden Jr., featuring patches from his four space missions, 1986–94.

This Medal of Honor was awarded posthumously to Sgt. Cornelius H. Charlton in 1952 for bravery during the Korean War.

Medal of Honor

The Medal of Honor is the nation's highest military award. In 1996, the Pentagon determined that some African Americans had been denied the medal because of race. During World War I and World War II, no African Americans received the medal, an oversight the Pentagon corrected in 1997.

This gallery features the stories of men who epitomized their nation's call for selfless service and the medal's requirements for "gallantry" and "actions above and beyond the call of duty." They include Sgt. Cornelius H. Charlton, who was killed in action while leading an assault on enemy forces during the Korean War; his Medal of Honor, awarded posthumously, is on display. Sgt. Charlton is one of several African American Medal of Honor recipients buried in Arlington National Cemetery, which can be viewed off in the distance through the window at the end of this gallery, beyond the Washington Monument and the Lincoln Memorial.

The gallery dedicated to African American Medal of Honor recipients offers a dramatic view of the Washington Monument.

GENEROUSLY SUPPORTED BY
THE BOEING COMPANY

African American
Medal of Honor
Recipients

The Medal of Honor (MOH) is the nation's highest military award. In 1996 the Pentagon determined that some African Americans had been denied the medal because of race. During World Wars I and II, no African Americans received the medal, an oversight the Pentagon corrected in 1997. The men in this gallery epitomized their nation's call for selfless service and the medal's requirements for "gallantry" and "actions above and beyond the call of duty." The brief quotations describing their bravery are excerpts from their Medal of Honor Citations. An asterisk (*) denotes medals awarded posthumously.

The black athlete, with ... superior skills and proud attitude, has become a dominant figure in the Negro struggle for equality.

—Ron Fair

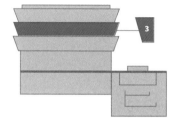

SPORTS

LEVELING THE PLAYING FIELD

Sports matter far beyond the playing field. Historically, African American athletes were denied opportunities to compete at the highest levels. Yet as one of the earliest public arenas to accept African Americans on terms of relative equality, sports have also served as a measuring stick for racial progress. Beyond the impressive records of individual achievements, the history of sports also demonstrates how African Americans have utilized sports to fight for greater rights and freedoms.

Sports: Leveling the Playing Field explores the role of sports as a vehicle for African American athletic performance, cultural expression, and political activism. Special sections focus on major sports and sporting events, including football, baseball, the Olympics, boxing, and basketball. Stories of the "Game Changers" examine the impact of individual athletes and athletic institutions on sports, culture, and society.

When African American athletes protested against racism at the 1968 Olympics, they demonstrated the impact of sports beyond the playing field.

Olympics

Since the first modern Olympics, in 1896, the Games have been an international stage on which to demonstrate superior athletic ability and display exemplary character and conduct. As African Americans fought prejudice at home, the Olympic Games provided an opportunity to challenge discrimination and racist views of black inferiority before a worldwide audience. From Jesse Owens's historic Nazi-defying victories at the 1936 Berlin Olympics to the current moment, African American Olympic athletes have sought to represent their country and to challenge it to live up to its highest ideals.

One of the most memorable and important protests against racism took place at the 1968 Olympic Games in Mexico City. After winning gold and bronze medals in the men's 200-meter sprint, U.S. athletes Tommie Smith and John Carlos mounted the ceremonial podium, bowed their heads, and raised their black-gloved fists while the national anthem played. The third athlete on the podium, white Australian Peter Norman, also participated in the protest, wearing an "Olympic Project for Human Rights" badge to signify his solidarity with Smith and Carlos. A statue at the entrance to the *Sports* gallery commemorates this pivotal moment. The warm-up suit that Tommie Smith wore on the podium in 1968 is also on display in this section.

Other objects representing the achievements of African American Olympians include nine of the ten Olympic medals won by track star Carl Lewis; the torch used by Rafer Johnson, the first African American to light the Olympic Flame, at the 1984 Olympics; a figure skating costume worn by Debi Thomas at the 1988 Winter Olympics; and track shoes worn by Mal Whitfield at the 1948 Olympics.

Olympic medals won by Carl Lewis in the men's 100-meter dash, 200-meter dash, 4 x 100-meter relay, and long jump, 1984–96.

Football

After launching as an integrated sport in 1920, professional football systematically excluded African Americans from the late 1920s through the end of World War II. At the collegiate level, African American sporting traditions strengthened during that time at historically black colleges and universities (HBCUs). Although the National Football League was the first of the major team sports to reintegrate, football has lagged far behind others in promoting African Americans into coaching and management positions.

The story of African Americans in college and professional football is told through artifacts such as an Ohio State Buckeyes helmet worn by Archie Griffin, the first and only college football player to win two Heisman trophies; a Cleveland Browns jersey worn by four-time NFL Most Valuable Player Jim Brown—considered by many to be the greatest football player of all time; and a spectacular Waterford crystal trophy awarded to the winner of the Bayou Classic, the annual game between two prestigious HBCU football teams, Grambling State and Southern University.

Warm-up suit worn by U.S. athlete and activist Tommie Smith during his protest at the 1968 Olympics in Mexico City.

Football helmet worn by Ohio State Buckeyes halfback and two-time Heisman Trophy winner Archie Griffin, 1972–75.

Basketball

In the early twentieth century, African Americans used men's and women's basketball to help instill middle-class values, promote good health, and campaign for racial uplift. Since then, basketball has become more closely identified with African American culture than any other mainstream sport. African American styles of play, evident since the early days of all-black teams like the New York Rens and the Harlem Globetrotters, have continued to influence the development of professional basketball over the past century. Slam-dunking, creative dribbling, and stylized play have been likened to the improvisational nature of African American music and other cultural forms.

Highlights in this section include a jersey worn by Earl Lloyd, the first African American to play in an NBA game; the autobiography of Bill Russell, the legendary center for the Boston Celtics who in 1966 became the first African American head coach in the NBA; and a jersey from the Washington Mystics, the WNBA team owned by Sheila Johnson, who is one of the few African American majority owners of a professional sports team.

The American Basketball Association (ABA), founded in 1967, put an innovative, freewheeling spin on the game and featured dynamic players like Julius "Dr. J." Erving.

Baseball

African Americans' long and complicated history with the "national pastime" has been marked by both exclusion and pioneering successes. The establishment of black baseball teams in the 1890s and the organization of the Negro Leagues in the 1920s created opportunities for African Americans to play the game professionally in a segregated nation. While the integration of Major League Baseball by Jackie Robinson in 1947 is one of the most significant events in the history of American sport, it also marked the demise of the Negro Leagues, which had been one of the

The baseball theater seats are modeled after originals from Griffith Stadium in Washington, D.C., which was home to the famous Homestead Grays in the 1940s.

biggest business institutions in black America. Meanwhile, integration of African Americans into the business and leadership sides of Major League Baseball lagged behind the integration of players on the field; not until 1974 did Frank Robinson became the first black manager of a Major League Baseball team. Despite the history of achievement and innovation that black players, coaches, and executives have brought to baseball, African American participation in the game has waned since the 1980s.

The story of the Negro Leagues as both a showcase for talented athletes and a black cultural and economic institution is told here through a variety of memorabilia, including a seat from Perry Stadium in Indianapolis, which served as home field for several Negro League teams. The achievements of African American players in Major League Baseball are evoked by objects such as a catcher's mitt worn by Roy Campanella, who played for the Brooklyn Dodgers along with Jackie Robinson; an Atlanta Braves jersey worn by home-run champion Hank Aaron; and a baseball bat used by Willie Mays in the 1965 All-Star Game. This section also features a theater, where you can sit on vintage-style stadium seats to watch a film about the history of African Americans and baseball.

Willie Mays, one of baseball's all-time greats, used this bat in the 1965 Major League Baseball All-Star Game.

Tennis and Golf

Even as more mainstream sports such as baseball, football, and basketball began to accept black competitors, golf and tennis remained closed to most African Americans. These sports helped convey social status, and players prided themselves on refined competition characterized by emotional control and gentlemanly and ladylike behavior. Because of these sports' close association with cultural elites, African American tennis players and golfers had to cross boundaries that were not present in other sports.

Althea Gibson, who broke barriers in professional tennis by becoming the first African American Grand Slam champion in 1957, was also the first African American woman to compete on the Ladies Professional Golf Association tour. The blazer Gibson wore at the prestigious Wightman Cup tennis tournament is on display here along with other objects from her pioneering career. Items from African American golfers include a golf bag used by United Golf Association national champion Ethel Funches and a Nike SasQuatch 460 driver used by golf champion Tiger Woods during PGA tournament play.

Muhammad Ali's boxing headgear, ca. 1973.

Boxing

Boxing and politics have been intertwined through much of the nation's history. Among African Americans, boxing's roots reach back to slavery, and a few fighters may have gained their freedom through success as boxers. In the 1800s, boxing was one of the most popular sports, and African Americans turned to "the sweet science" to challenge their enslavement and the racial discrimination of the Jim Crow era. Since then, African American fighters, promoters, trainers, and managers have used the sport to demonstrate courage, strategic thinking, and business acumen.

The first black world heavyweight boxing champion, Jack Johnson, won the title in 1908 after years of being denied a chance to compete. In 1910, he famously defended his title against Jim Jeffries, dubbed the "Great White Hope," and dealt an electrifying blow to racist notions of black inferiority. Fifty years later, a young contender named Cassius Clay, soon to be known as Muhammad Ali, rose to fame for his boxing prowess and his powerful social impact beyond the ring. Objects on display from these two outstanding black fighters include a carnival banner advertising Jack Johnson's boxing booth and a boxing robe and headgear worn by Ali while training at the 5th St. Gym in Miami.

Althea Gibson's Wightman Cup blazer, 1957.

The Michael Jordan Hall: Game Changers

At various moments in history, people, events, and institutions have forced the sports world and larger society to alter its practices, belief systems, or racial politics. Some of these shifts have led to the mainstreaming of African American cultural practices and the redefinition of gender roles, as well as a change in the racial composition of athletic institutions. The impact of these "Game Changers" demonstrates the power of sports to transform the world.

Stretching through the center of the *Sports* exhibition, a hall named for basketball superstar and philanthropist Michael Jordan pays dramatic tribute to athletes who changed the game. Featured individuals include baseball pioneer Jackie Robinson, track and field sprinter Wilma Rudolph, tennis icons Venus and Serena Williams, and the athlete, scholar, singer, and activist Paul Robeson. In addition to individual athletes, this section also highlights the collective contributions of African American jockeys to the sport of horseracing. Another case focuses on the impact of Title IX, the 1972 civil rights law prohibiting sex discrimination in federally funded education programs, which opened up new opportunities for African American women athletes to compete at both the collegiate and professional levels.

Throughout the exhibition, a series of displays entitled "Style Matters" explores how African American expressive culture has influenced the way sports are played, watched, and understood. These displays appear in the sections dedicated to football, basketball, and boxing, as well as in the Game Changers section. Through the creativity, charisma, and innovation that black athletes brought to the playing fields, they not only elevated sports to a performance but also claimed the freedom to express themselves in a society that had long denied that freedom to African Americans.

Game changers portrayed in The Michael Jordan Hall include the Williams sisters, Jesse Owens, and Jackie Robinson.

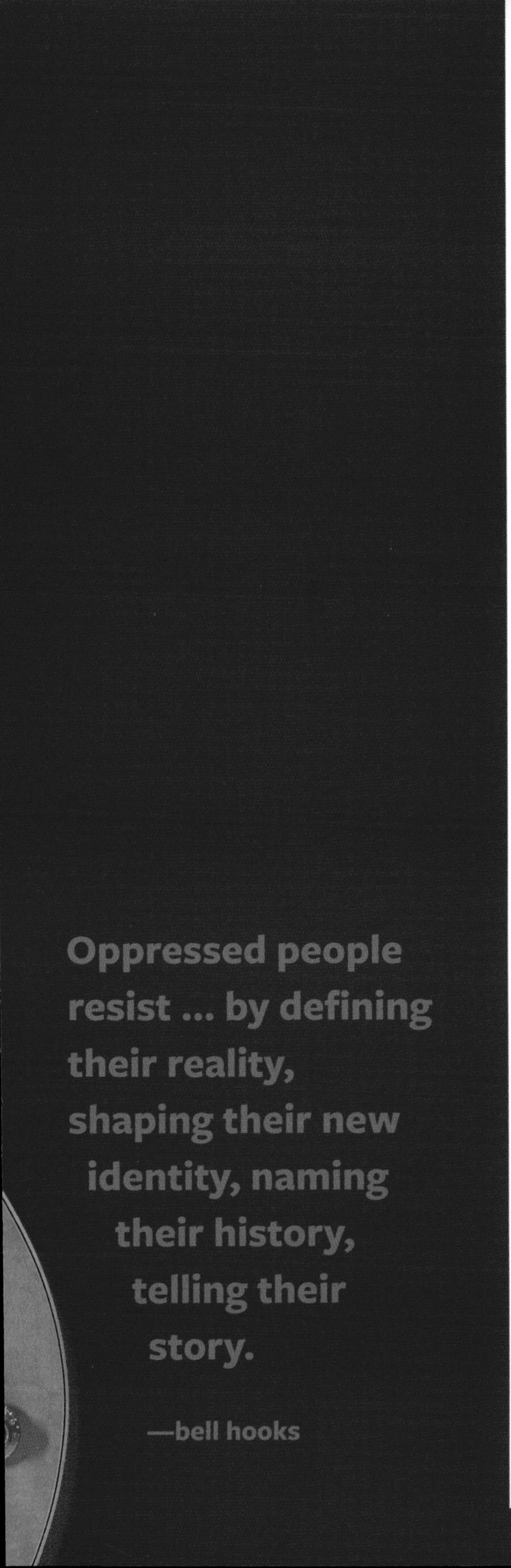

CULTURE GALLERIES

TRADITION AND INNOVATION

- 4 **CULTURAL EXPRESSIONS**
- 4 **MUSICAL CROSSROADS**
- 4 **TAKING THE STAGE**
- 4 **VISUAL ART AND THE AMERICAN EXPERIENCE**

Throughout history, African American culture has served as a tool for survival, a focus for creativity, a source of identity, and a force for change. Forged from traditions shared with other people of the African diaspora, African American culture has evolved through innovation, improvisation, and exchange and has embraced many different forms. The fourth floor of the National Museum of African American History and Culture is dedicated to exploring the wide spectrum of African American culture, from music and performing arts, painting, and sculpture, to language, fashion, and food.

Rock and roll legend Chuck Berry named this Gibson electric guitar "Maybellene," after his 1955 hit song.

Oppressed people resist ... by defining their reality, shaping their new identity, naming their history, telling their story.

—bell hooks

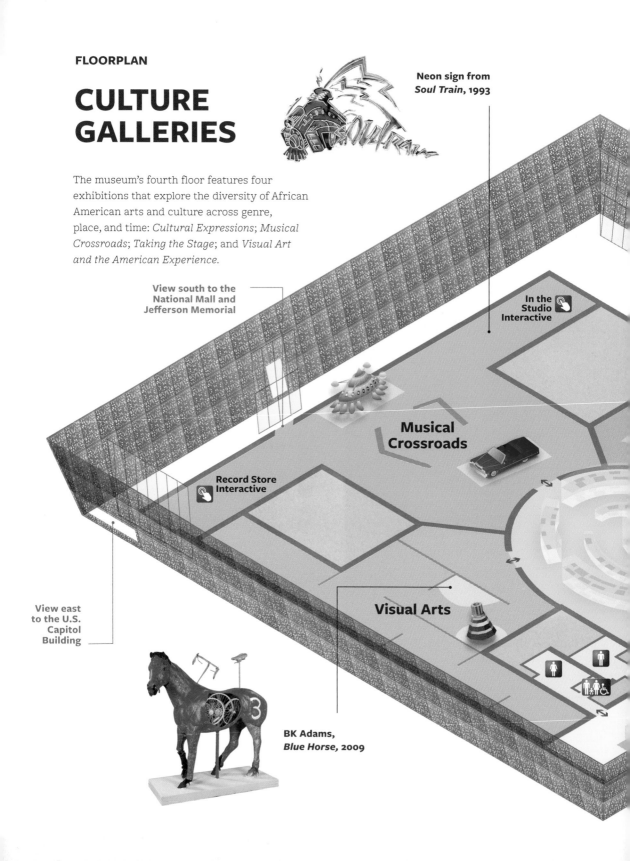

FLOORPLAN

CULTURE GALLERIES

The museum's fourth floor features four exhibitions that explore the diversity of African American arts and culture across genre, place, and time: *Cultural Expressions*; *Musical Crossroads*; *Taking the Stage*; and *Visual Art and the American Experience*.

Neon sign from
***Soul Train*, 1993**

View south to the National Mall and Jefferson Memorial

In the Studio Interactive

Musical Crossroads

Record Store Interactive

View east to the U.S. Capitol Building

Visual Arts

BK Adams,
***Blue Horse,* 2009**

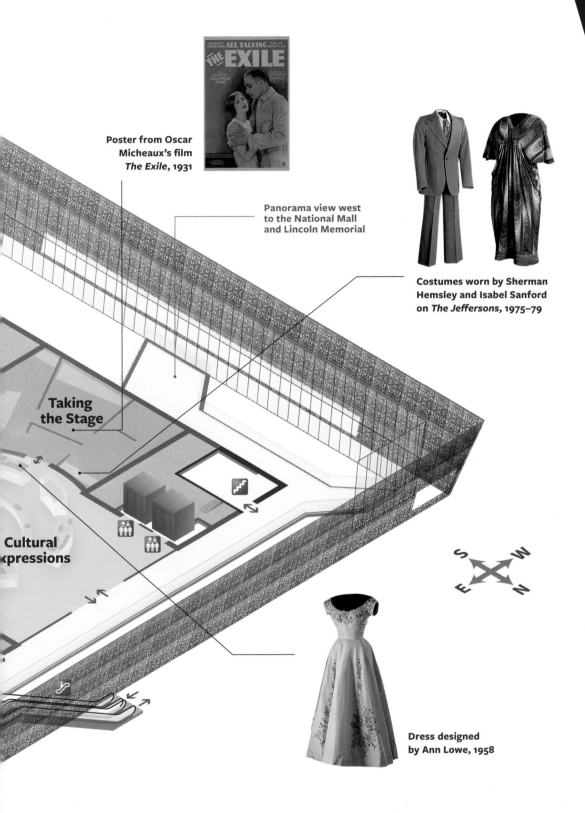

Poster from Oscar Micheaux's film *The Exile*, 1931

Panorama view west to the National Mall and Lincoln Memorial

Costumes worn by Sherman Hemsley and Isabel Sanford on *The Jeffersons*, 1975–79

Taking the Stage

Cultural Expressions

Dress designed by Ann Lowe, 1958

THE ARTS . . . FEED THE SPIRIT . . . FEED THE SOUL . . .
EDUCATE IN AREAS THAT BOOKS DON'T.
BETYE SAAR

Wherever I go,
I bring the
culture with me.

—Jay-Z

CULTURAL EXPRESSIONS

As you arrive on the museum's fourth floor, *Cultural Expressions* surrounds you with the vibrant sights, sounds, and textures of African American culture. Exhibition sections, arranged in a colorful patchwork of curved cases, explore five different forms of African American cultural expression: style, movement, foodways, artistry, and language. The central space, the Cultural Commons, examines cultural connections between African Americans and other people of the African diaspora. Overhead, a 360-degree media projection presents a kaleidoscope of images, music, and words that evoke the richness and diversity of African American culture.

The exhibition also features a bottle tree, created by contemporary artist Stephanie Dwyer in homage to a traditional practice brought to the American South by enslaved Africans, and a rotating display of quilts from the museum's collection that reflect the diversity of African American quilting traditions, patterns, and styles.

A sculpture by Olowe of Ise, a Yoruba artist, is a focal point of the *Cultural Expressions* gallery.

Cultural Commons

African diaspora people have a complex relationship with their African roots. African families and groups, separated in the Transatlantic Slave Trade, lost some important links to who they were. But African Americans still use Africa, African culture, and African art as badges—symbols of pride that link them to their cultural heritage. Across the diaspora, shared origins and freedom struggles have also fostered cultural similarities among African American, Afro-Caribbean, and Afro-Latin people.

In the center of the *Cultural Expressions* gallery, the significance of Africa as a cultural source for African Americans and other people of the African diaspora is symbolized by a striking work of art—a wooden veranda post, carved by Nigerian sculptor Olowe of Ise, which served as one of the inspirations for the architects who designed the museum. The carving depicts a priest mounted on a horse, topped by a crown-like form that is echoed in the tiered structure of the building's façade.

Spreading out from this symbolic figure, a ring of cases explores cultural traditions and connections among African diaspora people. Highlights include a colorful Madras headdress from the island of Guadeloupe—a contemporary expression of a tradition dating back to the 1700s and 1800s, when French colonial dress codes prohibited women of color from wearing hats —and a wooden boat seat from Ecuador, carved with the image of Anansi the spider, a character from African and African diaspora folktales. Deborah Azareno, an Afro-Ecuadorean woman, spun stories for her grandchildren while sitting on the seat, which was the first object collected by the museum, donated in 2005 by her grandson.

Moving out from the Cultural Commons, the exhibition continues along the outer ring of cases, which explores five different types of African American cultural expression.

Artistry: Craftsmanship and Creativity

Black artists and craftspeople express culture in distinct and fascinating ways. The work they create can stretch back into the past, reflect the present, or lean toward an imagined future. Some embrace a connection to African or African American culture. Others call out different cultural influences. Master artists, working in both traditional and non-traditional mediums, display skills acquired through training and

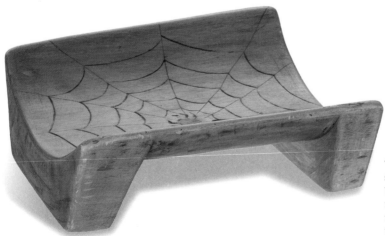

The image of Anansi the spider on this Ecuadorean boat seat of the early 1900s evokes storytelling traditions shared across the African diaspora.

honed through years of practice. From wrought-iron gates to modernist jewelry, from woven baskets to subway graffiti, African American artistry expresses both a collective cultural history and the artists' personal experience.

This section displays examples of work created by master artisans such as Philip Simmons, a blacksmith whose ornamental wrought-iron gates are signature elements of the landscape of his native city of Charleston, South Carolina. Another South Carolina artist, Mary Jackson, draws upon the basket-making traditions brought to rice and cotton plantations by enslaved Africans to craft her modern designs that evoke a connection to this past. Her grain-storage basket, made from bulrush and oak strips, recalls the baskets historically made by black men in the Lowcountry. Also on view are several pieces of jewelry made by Art Smith, including a striking copper and brass bracelet. From his Greenwich

Modernist jeweler Art Smith designed this elegant copper and brass bracelet, titled *Modern Cuff*, around 1948.

Village studio and shop, Smith, a leading figure of the mid-twentieth-century modernist jewelry movement, designed "wearable art" for modern dance companies, famous clients such as Duke Ellington and Eleanor Roosevelt, and the liberal avant-garde.

Language: The Power of Words

Rapping, preaching, testifying, storytelling, signifying, playing the dozens—at its heart, African American culture is an oral culture. As enslaved Africans combined English with their native vocabularies and ways of talking, they created a language that built communities and kept them going. Talking and telling connect people to each other and to a shared history. Styles of speech and choices of words change depending on context and intention.

Objects, images, and video in this section reflect the many different ways language is expressed and used in the African American community. A horn used to signal the start of religious revival meetings at Shady Grove, a United Methodist campground in South Carolina, bears witness to African American preaching traditions, while

An iron gate crafted by Charleston blacksmith Philip Simmons in the 1970s fuses art and function.

a 1967 trophy awarded to the Texas Southern University Debate Team represents how students at historically black colleges and universities (HBCUs) used language as an educational and political tool for dismantling notions of African American inferiority. *Coded Language*, a handwritten scroll created by slam poet Saul Williams, and the works of other poets such as Nikki Finney and Lucille Clifton, evoke the power of poetry and the spoken word.

Style: Image and Identity

Style is an expression of African American culture, identity, and community. For over two centuries, black Americans lived in a world that saw their skin, hair, and other physical features as ugly. In response, African American styles have imitated white beauty standards, woven in black cultural values, or rejected white standards entirely. In recent years, images celebrating the beauty and diversity of African Americans have gained wider cultural acceptance.

In this section of *Cultural Expressions*, objects and images reflect how African Americans have used clothing, skin color, and hairstyles to express and redefine ideas of beauty and status. Examples of how clothing can make powerful cultural and political statements include a silk cocktail dress designed by pioneering designer Ann Lowe, a 1960s' dashiki, and a cap worn by hip-hop artist Kangol Kid. The painful history of "colorism"—discrimination against people based on the lightness or darkness of their skin—is explored through a video and an interactive based on the infamous "paper-bag test" that many African American social organizations used to exclude darker-skinned individuals. Along with dark skin, natural hair has carried both negative and positive associations in African American culture. The weight of this history is imaginatively evoked by artist Kenya (Robinson) in *Commemorative Headdress of Her Journey Beyond Heaven*, a crown-like sculpture assembled from dozens of plastic hair combs.

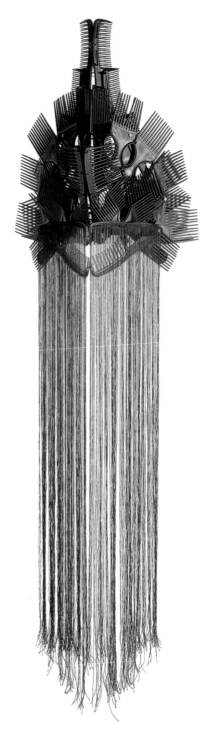

Kenya (Robinson), *Commemorative Headdress of Her Journey Beyond Heaven*, 2010.

Movement: Gesture and Social Dance

In African American culture, the movement of the body is a complex and powerful language all its own. Everyday gestures communicate a range of messages and emotions. Improvised dances at social gatherings express a sense of community as well as the distinctive personalities and skills of the dancers.

In this section, a collage of images reflects the variety of gestures developed and used by African Americans that have become part of the lexicon of American culture. They include gestures of solidarity—from the "dap," exchanged by black soldiers in Vietnam to demonstrate brotherhood and pride, to the "fist bump" of today—as well as gestures of play, such as double dutch and handclapping games, and gestures of praise and protest. Also featured in the Movement section is a video chronicling the history of African American social dances. From the cakewalk to the Dougie, these dances have expressed cultural traditions, reflected social change, and shaped the way all Americans move to the beat.

Foodways: Culture and Cuisine

Food is central to African American culture, encompassing not only what people eat but also how they grow and prepare it, and the various roles that food plays in their lives. Africans brought with them planting and cooking techniques and memories of recipes. Enslaved and free African Americans cooked in the kitchens of white families, restaurants, and even the White House. Over the past century, many found jobs in food service, in places as varied as boarding houses, hotels, cattle ranches, and Pullman cars. Today, a new generation of black chefs continues to contribute to the evolution of American cuisine.

Among the many objects on display that help tell the story of African American foodways are a pot used to cook greens at the Florida Avenue Grill in Washington, D.C., which bills itself as "the oldest soul food restaurant in the world"; a wire basket used by Maryland watermen to harvest oysters on the Chesapeake Bay; and a red chef's jacket worn by the Queen of Creole cuisine, Leah Chase, at her landmark New Orleans restaurant, Dooky Chase's. (Be sure to visit the museum's Sweet Home Café, where you can learn more about the history of African American cuisine and sample some of these delicious food traditions for yourself!)

The Queen of Creole Cuisine, Leah Chase, expressed her flavorful style with this brightly colored chef's jacket, ca. 2012.

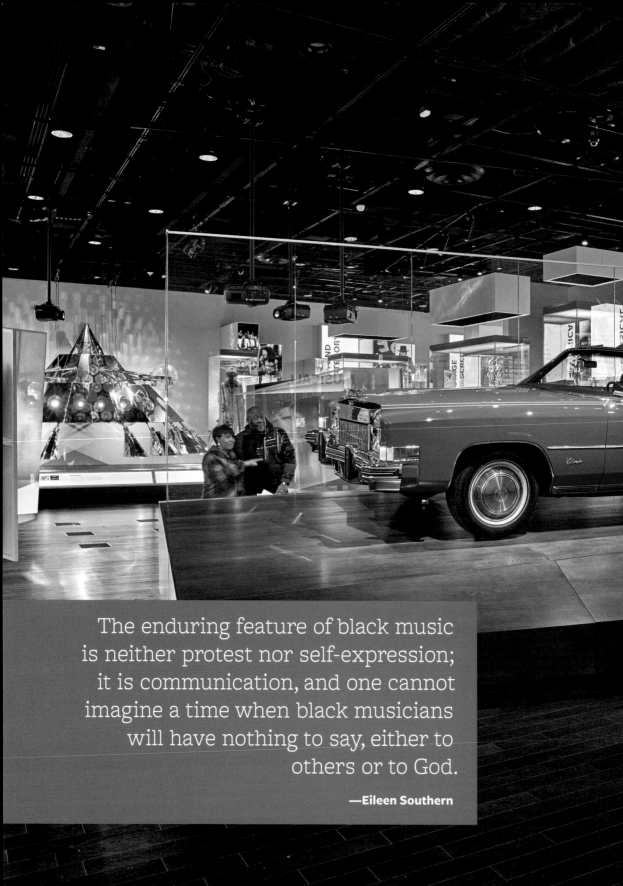

The enduring feature of black music is neither protest nor self-expression; it is communication, and one cannot imagine a time when black musicians will have nothing to say, either to others or to God.

—**Eileen Southern**

MUSICAL CROSSROADS

The arrival of the first Africans on these shores set a new path for American music. For more than four hundred years, African American musical creativity and innovation have generated, transformed, and enriched a vast array of musical forms. From blues and country, to jazz and funk, to classical and rock and roll, the musical creations of African Americans have woven a narrative of hope and struggle, faith and perseverance, culture and tradition, and pride and liberation.

Musical Crossroads explores the history and culture of African American music through a captivating array of artifacts, images, and sounds, which are organized by musical styles and related themes. At the entrance, a red Cadillac Eldorado owned by Chuck Berry evokes the sense of freedom, exuberance, and innovation that defined rock and roll. At the center of the gallery, an immersive video features performances by African American musicians across time and genre.

Chuck Berry's 1973 Cadillac Eldorado welcomes visitors to the *Musical Crossroads* exhibition.

The Roots of African American Music

The story of African American music begins in Africa. Enslaved Africans from across the continent brought with them a wide range of cultural traditions and performance practices. Music functioned in African cultures as a means of communication and creative expression, and as a collective experience that blurred the line between performers and audience and emphasized unity and group consciousness. Traditional African musical performances were also multisensory and multidimensional, combining rhythmic contrasts and percussion, body movements, and tonal patterns, speech, chant, and song. By preserving their musical traditions and techniques amid the drastic changes of surroundings and circumstances, enslaved Africans created the template of unique sounds that redefined the basis of American music.

An introductory video in this first section explores the social and cultural context of more than four hundred years of African American music and music making. Also on display are images of African percussion, wind, and string instruments, several of which are ancestors of instruments we know today, and a colorfully decorated Rada drum from Haiti, which speaks to the cultural significance of drumming in African diaspora communities.

Folk, Blues, and Country

A similar musical language links folk, blues, and country. Together, they express the hopes, sorrows, and convictions of ordinary people. Through these genres, African Americans have passed on African cultural traditions, spurred new musical innovations, and protested the effects of racial oppression and social injustice.

Folk music has been used to tell countless American stories of struggle, empowerment, and perseverance, and African Americans have made immeasurable contributions to those stories. From early spirituals to the protest music of the 1960s and present-day hip-hop, folk songs blur the category lines to provide a musical voice for the community. The blues, which is the foundation for most genres of modern American popular music, is also the soundtrack of Jim Crow America, narrating the ups and downs of life and

Country music star Charley Pride wore this outfit on the cover of his 1976 greatest-hits album.

the experiences of African Americans living in segregated communities. The blues also marks the period when secular themes and expressions began to vigorously shape the sound and content of American music. Country music, like any other style, is an intersection of musical ideas and innovations that crosses racial lines. African Americans have created, played, and listened to country music since its beginnings—and drawn inspiration from its old-time traditions. Featured artifacts that illustrate the contributions of African Americans to folk, blues, and country include a 1937 Stella 12-string acoustic guitar played by legendary folk and blues musician Huddie Ledbetter, better known as Lead Belly, a caftan worn by Odetta, an influential folk singer of the Civil Rights Movement, and a denim outfit worn by country superstar Charley Pride.

This section also explores the history of the banjo, one of the most important folk instruments in American culture. While popularly associated with white Appalachian culture, the banjo is rooted in African, Afro-Caribbean, and African American cultures. Its transformation over the centuries—from the banjar, a gourd instrument brought to the Americas by enslaved West Africans, to the stereotypical banjo players of the nineteenth-century blackface minstrel shows, to the versatile instrument played by musicians in a wide variety of styles, from ragtime and jazz to roots and blues—represents a very American story of cultural contact and innovation.

R&B and Soul

Though used as a blanket term for popular African American music since the 1940s, rhythm and blues (R&B) also signifies the beat-driven dance music that originated from jazz, blues, and gospel and helped to shape the sounds of rock, soul, funk, and hip-hop. R&B developed across different regions and incorporated varied sounds and structures—from boogie-woogie piano stylings and hard-swinging jump blues to ballads and a cappella vocals. Since the 1980s,

contemporary R&B has continued to evolve, borrowing back from genres such as funk and hip-hop and incorporating electronic beats and sounds, while also remaining true to its popular roots.

Soul music emerged from the artistic groundwork of gospel and rhythm and blues to become popular music's soundtrack for the pride

Jermaine Jackson wore this costume during a Jackson 5 performance at the London Palladium in 1972.

Antoine "Fats" Domino Jr., one of R&B's first icons, wore these shoes (late 1900s).

and protest movements of the 1960s and 1970s. Frequently used interchangeably with R&B, soul stands out as a musical style that focuses on the importance of feel and emotional connectivity within the music. Soul draws from its gospel roots while sonically and lyrically endorsing larger themes of protest, including racial pride, Black Power, and social injustice.

The history of these two enormously popular and influential kinds of music is represented here by artifacts such as an original manuscript for Louis Jordan's 1944 Top 10 hit "Is You Is or Is You Ain't My Baby"; a pair of shoes worn by New Orleans R&B artist Fats Domino; a costume worn onstage in 1972 by Jermaine Jackson of the Jackson 5; and one of the costumes worn by En Vogue in the music video for the vocal group's 1992 single "Giving Him Something He Can Feel."

Rock and Roll

Before Elvis Presley recorded his first single at Sun Records in 1954, black musicians had already drafted the blueprint for the music that would soon take over the world. Rock and roll was the product of a cross-cultural fusion that combined American popular song structure with the sounds of African American sacred and secular music, including gospel, jazz, blues, and rhythm and blues. The resulting sound was fresh, different, and decidedly modern. With its aggressive rhythms, electric instrumentation, and tumultuous performances, rock and roll evoked the spirit of teenage rebellion and embodied the definition of cool. It also created a space for African American artists to express musical identities that challenged and transcended racial categories.

Among the classic rock and roll artifacts on view here are a blue beaded jacket worn by the innovative and inimitable Little Richard; Chuck Berry's Gibson guitar—nicknamed "Maybellene," after his first hit song; the original 1952 recording of "Hound Dog" performed by Willie Mae "Big Mama" Thornton; and a vest worn by trailblazing rock guitarist Jimi Hendrix. A hat worn by H.R. (Paul Hudson), lead singer of the influential hardcore punk band Bad Brains, and a bass guitar played by Norwood Fisher, a member of the eclectic rock-punk-funk-ska band Fishbone, represent the continuing ways in which African American artists have challenged, expanded, and redefined the boundaries of the rock genre.

Jimi Hendrix, an artist renowned for his eclectic and electric style, wore this vest during the 1960s.

Global Impact and Influence

Music of the African diaspora is central to African American music. From the Caribbean and Latin America to Europe and even some parts of Asia, the circle of musical voices that make up this African diaspora is the most lasting sign of the connection among people of African descent. These communities have been a source of musical creativity for more than four hundred years. Their music represents a broad sweep of musical traditions and new sounds with deep roots in Africa.

As African American artists have drawn musical and cultural influences from around the globe, they also continue to disseminate African American music and culture to a global community. Much of what the world has learned about the United States has been through African American music. The music's dynamic elements of transcendence and liberation projected American principles of self-determination, freedom, and democracy abroad even as African Americans struggled to achieve those very things at home.

Artifacts that help tell this story of global impact and influence include a piece of sheet music for the 1930 song "J'ai Deux Amours (I Have Two Loves)," performed by dancer, singer, activist, and international sensation Josephine Baker; a travel permit used by composer and choir conductor Hall Johnson during a European tour; and a sequined dress worn by Cuban singer Celia Cruz, known as the Queen of Salsa.

Hip-Hop and Rap

Since its emergence in the 1970s, hip-hop culture has grown from a relatively small community into a major international sociocultural and economic phenomenon. The foundation was laid by a multicultural group of graffiti artists, DJs, MCs, b-boys, and b-girls who came together in the South Bronx, New York, amid poverty and unrest to collaborate in the spirit of peace, unity, and celebration. As they experimented with new styles of playing records and pulling sounds and beats from multiple musical genres, they generated a revolutionary energy that would redefine the landscape of American music.

Rap, which has functioned as both an offshoot and integral part of hip-hop music and culture, was born when the first DJs stepped from behind

Queen of Salsa, the Cuban singer and entertainer Celia Cruz, wore this colorful dress in one of her 1970s stage performances.

Track sheet for Queen Latifah's feminist hip-hop anthem "Ladies First," produced by DJ Mark the 45 King, 1989.

and musical style, hip-hop has seemed at times to celebrate hyper-masculinity, sexual promiscuity, and misogyny. Many women hip-hop and rap performers have challenged these images through self-empowering lyrics, feminist ideology, and their supremely independent stage personas. As a style that continues to embrace and build upon its cross-cultural foundations—from the Bronx to East Asia—hip-hop undeniably shapes modern-day popular music and culture and continues to transcend race, class, and nationality.

This section explores the history and impact of hip-hop culture through significant artifacts such as a leather jacket worn by the rapper Kurtis Blow; a track sheet for the recording of "Ladies First," performed by Queen Latifah and Monie Love; and electronic musical instruments used by legendary hip-hop producer J Dilla.

their turntables with a microphone. Combining poetry and spoken word with elaborate storytelling in the tradition of African griots, rapping became a vehicle for MCs to speak their minds about the cultural, social, and political happenings of the time. By the mid-1990s, the emergence of two new subgenres of rap—gangsta and "message" or "conscious" rap—pushed the music to ever-greater popularity but also supplanted its quirky and original flavor with a more mass-produced sound.

Hip-hop and rap are among the most popular forms of music in the world, but they are not without conflict and controversy. As a culture

Music of a City: Go-Go and Washington, D.C.

Go-go has been the soundtrack of Washington, D.C., since the 1970s—born here and heard throughout the city, in clubs and on street corners, like early jazz in New Orleans. A subgenre of funk with strong ties to rhythm and blues, hip-hop, and Latin music, go-go is

Hip-hop producer J Dilla used this Minimoog Voyager synthesizer (left) and Akai MIDI Production Center (right) to create his signature sounds (early 2000s).

characterized by its unique rhythm, or "go-go swing." Street drummers pound out the go-go beat on overturned buckets, while go-go bands create percussive layers with congas, cowbells, and roto tom drums, punctuated bursts from the brass section, and improvised call and response between singer and audience. Over the years, go-go has survived and evolved through the sheer will and grassroots efforts of its artists and dedicated fans. A suit worn by Chuck Brown, known as the Godfather of Go-Go, and a hand conga played by members of the go-go band Experience Unlimited (E.U.) are among the artifacts on display here to represent the artistry and spirit of this homegrown music scene.

One Nation Under a Groove: Funk and Dance Music

Emerging just after the Civil Rights Movement, funk was the ultimate musical hybrid, taking its musical cues from blues, rock, R&B, and soul music as well as gospel and jazz. The pioneer of funk was soul singer James Brown, whose band developed a dance-oriented style built around a central, pulsating rhythm that emphasized the first beat of every measure, called "the one." Brown's profound impact on popular music as a singer, songwriter, and showman is represented by various artifacts throughout the *Musical Crossroads* exhibition, including a black "Sex" jumpsuit worn during one of his signature high-energy stage performances.

As the mastermind of Parliament, Funkadelic, and the musical collective known as P-Funk, George Clinton fused disparate musical ideas to produce a completely original sound. To complement the spirit of the music, Clinton and his band members created spectacular, psychedelic stage shows. The P-Funk Mothership, the centerpiece of these space-age funk operas, became one of the most famous props in the history of popular music; the version on display here dates from the 1990s.

James Brown, the Godfather of Soul, wore this black jumpsuit with "SEX" spelled out in rhinestones (1970s).

THE MOTHERSHIP CONNECTION

George Clinton performing with Parliament-Funkadelic.

Swing down, sweet chariot
Stop and let me ride

—Parliament,
"Mothership Connection
(Star Child)," 1975

Among the many evocative objects collected by the museum to tell the story of African American music, one literally hovers above the rest. The P-Funk Mothership first appeared on the cover of Parliament's 1975 futuristic concept album, *Mothership Connection*, taking funk bandmaster George Clinton on a fantastic voyage through outer space. Over the next two decades, Clinton and his band would invite concert audiences to join them for the ride, as the Mothership, summoned by the force of the funk, landed onstage in a cloud of smoke and flashing lights during their live shows.

In 2010, hoping to acquire this legendary piece of music history for the Smithsonian, curators went in search of the Mothership. While the original had long since left this earthly plane, a nearly exact replica had been created for the Mothership Reconnection Tour in the 1990s. With Clinton's blessing, this new Mothership made its final voyage to the museum, where it was reassembled and installed in all its glowing, intergalactic glory for the *Musical Crossroads* exhibition. A time capsule for fans to relive their P-Funk memories, the Mothership is also an enduring and uplifting symbol of the liberating power of music.

The P-Funk Mothership on display in *Musical Crossroads,* flanked by costumes worn by band leader George Clinton and bassist Bootsy Collins.

Beyond Category

Many African American musicians have simultaneously been innovators and revolutionaries, whose lives and music eclipse racial and artistic categories. From Paul Robeson to Public Enemy, black artists have often used music as a form of activism. In raising their voices to oppose racism, violence, and oppression in all its forms, they conveyed messages of solidarity and protest that crossed racial and national lines and demonstrated that a musician's influence could reach far beyond the stage. Others, such as Duke Ellington and Michael Jackson, went beyond category by creating original music that defined a historical moment, an entire era, or even a genre. Their work has not only stood the test of time but also provided the foundation for further artistic inspiration and innovation by musicians everywhere, regardless of musical style. Some artists, like jazz legend Miles Davis, carried innovation to a whole new level, not only changing the sound but challenging the rules and structures of music itself in the pursuit of creative expression and artistic truth.

The King of Pop, Michael Jackson, wore this black sequined jacket during The Jacksons' 1984 Victory Tour.

For artists in the music industry, exploration and innovation became tools for crossing over into new markets and reaching larger audiences. By blurring the invisible but very real lines that divide music and marketing by racial categories, crossover artists such as Ethel Waters, Sammy Davis Jr., and Whitney Houston redefined how music is listened to and sold.

Objects on display that represent the musical styles and achievements of boundary-breaking artists include a sequined jacket worn by Michael Jackson during The Jacksons' 1984 Victory Tour; a pair of child's tap shoes worn by Sammy Davis Jr., who began his show business career at the age of three; and a red designer gown worn by Whitney Houston when she performed "I Have Nothing" at the Billboard Music Awards in 1993.

Music on Stage and Screen

The history of African American music on the stage and screen begins with America's first popular form of theatrical entertainment, the minstrel show. Originally performed by white actors in blackface, the songs, dances, and skits of the minstrel show presented a caricature of black life that appealed to white audiences' fascination with African American culture while also reinforcing racist views of black inferiority. Ironically, the popularity of minstrel shows opened the stage door to black musical and theatrical performers, who then went on to create new productions that showcased African American music in more innovative and authentic ways.

As minstrelsy declined in popularity at the turn of the twentieth century, vaudeville began to flourish. Vaudeville shows included music, novelty acts, sketches, and short plays and provided essential training for African American musicians and performers. Most of the artists performed on the Theater Owners Booking Association (TOBA) circuit, a network of predominantly white-owned theaters in black areas of towns across much of the country. Black vaudeville helped

launch the careers of singers, composers, and instrumentalists who went on to greater success in jazz, blues, and musical theater. The vaudeville circuit in turn gave way to the so-called chitlin' circuit, which brought a steady stream of traveling blues, jazz, and R&B musicians to clubs, theaters, and other venues that catered to black audiences.

With the advent of film and television, African American musicians gained more opportunities to perform for larger audiences. But they also continued to struggle against racial discrimination and stereotypes rooted in the minstrel shows of the 1800s. Up through the 1950s, Hollywood films often restricted appearances by black artists to a musical or dance number (usually set on a plantation or at a nightclub) that could easily be edited out to appease white audiences in the segregated South. Television, on the other hand,

brought black performers directly into America's living rooms. Through appearances on talk, variety, dance, and music shows, black artists and the entire culture of African American music began to dominate popular entertainment.

The story of African American musical performance on the stage and screen is illustrated here through objects such as a tiple played by singer and stand-up comedian Timmie Rogers, who performed at the Apollo Theater in New York and on television variety shows during the 1950s and 1960s; a costume worn by Diana Ross as Billie Holiday in the 1972 film *Lady Sings the Blues*; and a neon sign from the set of *Soul Train*, the syndicated television show created by Don Cornelius that became a showcase for African American popular music and a cultural phenomenon.

Jazz and Syncopated Instrumental

Jazz is a foundational sound of American music. Derived from the syncopated instrumental styles of ragtime and stride piano playing, jazz emerged in New Orleans in the early 1920s and flowed with the Great Migration to cities like Kansas City, Chicago, and New York, where it took root and flourished. As jazz evolved, its exploratory, improvisational, and innovative techniques provided a unique voice for black cultural expression and laid the blueprint for much of modern American popular music.

The lifeblood of jazz during the 1920s and 1930s was "swing"—a strong rhythmic drive complemented by a call and response between different sections in a band. Big bands ruled the day, with one to two dozen musicians and full sections of rhythm, brass, and woodwind. Although some bands were partially integrated, most were split along racial lines. Black musicians such as Chick Webb, Fletcher Henderson, Don Redman, Jimmie Lunceford, and Cab Calloway led some of the most popular big bands of the swing era.

While bandleaders supplied the defining rhythm of jazz, vocalists used rhythmic and melodic variations to reinterpret songs in unique ways. Singers like Sarah Vaughan, Billie Holiday, and Ella Fitzgerald pioneered new ways of manipulating phrasing and tempo to give songs special meaning. Like instrumentalists, the singers also improvised, contributing new sounds and styles to the history of jazz.

Legendary jazz artist Louis Armstrong played this custom-made B-flat trumpet during the late 1940s.

During the 1940s, musicians broke away from traditional swing and began to cultivate and showcase their own improvisational technique. Bebop pioneers such as trumpet player Dizzy Gillespie and saxophonist Charlie "Bird" Parker helped create a modern jazz style that highlighted improvised explorations of harmonic structure and melody. By the late 1950s, artists such as Miles Davis and John Coltrane had moved beyond bop jazz, which largely relied on soloing over fixed chord progressions, to a modal approach that used altered scales to expand the musical potential for the soloist. The free and fusion jazz that followed would take these steps even further, expanding on the language and sonic possibilities of jazz.

Legendary figures in jazz history are evoked here through objects such as a trumpet played by Louis "Satchmo" Armstrong; a tuxedo worn by singer and bandleader Cab Calloway; a dress worn by Ella Fitzgerald, "First Lady of Song"; a 1952 acetate disc recording by Billie Holiday; and a bass guitar played by electric jazz pioneer Stanley Clarke.

In the Classical Tradition

As classical musicians, African Americans have not only mastered traditional European musical forms but also infused them with their own aesthetic values. Through their artistry and accomplishments, these musicians have revealed how art transcends ethnic considerations and demonstrated the creative freedom of drawing from many traditions to express a personal artistic vision.

Beginning in the mid-1800s, African Americans found more opportunities to study classical music as churches, historically black colleges and universities (HBCUs), and music schools began to provide training for them. Free men and women also developed a concert life in their communities through choral clubs, music societies, and programs at black churches. Many black musicians and community leaders believed that studying classical music would uplift the race and prove that African Americans had the intelligence and skill to master this high art form. But in presenting their art on the concert stage, African American composers, instrumentalists, and vocalists faced intense scrutiny and racist attitudes from those who doubted their ability to perform music from European traditions.

Highlights in this section include a flute owned by Thomas "Blind Tom" Wiggins, one of the most popular composers and entertainers of the 1800s; a broadside from an 1876 performance by the Hyers Sisters, two concert singers who formed a professional musical theater company to showcase the talents of black performing artists; and clothing associated with singer Marian Anderson's famous Easter Sunday concert at the Lincoln Memorial in 1939.

In the Spirit: Sacred Music Traditions

For generations, African American sacred music has provided spiritual comfort, preserved cultural traditions, and communicated messages of survival and triumph in the face of oppression. Incorporating a wide variety of performance traditions, it has sustained people inside and outside the church and brought hope for salvation and liberation to communities worldwide.

The folk spiritual is the earliest form of African American music. Along with other African worship practices, such as the ring shout, spirituals were an integral part of the "invisible church" in which enslaved people developed and practiced their faith traditions, often in secret or remote locations. By the late 1800s, formally arranged versions of folk spirituals were being performed in American concert halls by groups like the Fisk Jubilee Singers.

Beginning in the late 1700s, African American Christians developed their own religious institutions, including Methodist, Baptist, and Pentecostal denominations. Some of these churches used folk spirituals in their services, but congregations also composed new hymns that incorporated traditional European arrangements as well as other musical forms.

Rooted in the spirituals and gospel hymns of the black church, gospel music emerged in the twentieth century in urban working-class communities and was widely popularized by gospel musicians such as Thomas Dorsey, Charles Albert Tindley, Rosetta Tharpe, Mahalia Jackson, the Clara Ward Singers, and the Dixie Hummingbirds. The music continued to evolve

Marian Anderson wore this ensemble (modified in 1993) when she performed at the Lincoln Memorial in 1939.

during the 1960s and 1970s, embracing a range of styles and greater instrumentation, including electronic instruments. Today, gospel music has become a global industry, reaching a worldwide market through publicity, recordings, and concerts. The appeal of gospel, in its traditional and modern versions, has always been partly religious and partly secular, a sacred message presented through compelling music.

The history and diversity of African American sacred music traditions are represented here by objects such as a piano from Pilgrim Baptist Church in Chicago used by composer and choir director Thomas Dorsey—the "father of gospel music"; an electric console steel guitar built and played by Detroit-based Felton Williams Jr.; and a Grammy Award received by the renowned southern black gospel quartet the Dixie Hummingbirds.

Getting the Music Heard: African Americans and the Music Industry

As songwriters, recording artists, music publishers, promoters, and entrepreneurs, African Americans have carved out a place as creative and successful leaders in the music industry. In the process, they participated in a cultural and commercial exchange that enriched American popular music and spread African American music around the world.

The Neighborhood Record Store features racks of album covers and an interactive table that plays musical selections.

Among the objects on display in this section are an early 78-rpm record released by Black Swan, the first record label primarily owned and operated by African Americans; a neon sign from Minton's Playhouse, the Harlem club that gave birth to bebop; a shag-carpet-insulated door from the office of music producer Thom Bell at Philadelphia International Records, the company that defined the soul music sound of the 1970s; and a Platinum Record Award presented to Prince for selling more than one million copies of his album *1999*.

You can get a behind-the-scenes experience of the music industry by checking out "In the Studio," an interactive that invites you to participate in a virtual recording session by sampling beats, melodies, and harmonies to produce your own song. This section also features a video tour of the studio of music producer and record company executive, 9th Wonder.

Neighborhood Record Store

In African American communities, neighborhood record stores were places where black entrepreneurship, commerce, and community came together. They provided safe spaces where people could engage with the music and with each other. In this special section of *Musical Crossroads*, you can browse racks of record albums, listen to songs, and relive your own musical memories in a setting that evokes a traditional neighborhood record store. In the center of the space, a touch-screen table offers an interactive way to explore African American music by learning more about your favorite songs and tracing relationships and influences across different styles, regions, and time periods. The interactive also lets you select excerpts of songs to play in the record store gallery.

Vinyl records, album covers, posters, and contracts document the history of African Americans in the music industry.

What the black actor has managed to give are moments—indelible moments, created, miraculously, beyond the confines of the script: hints of reality, smuggled like contraband into a maudlin tale, and with enough force, if unleashed, to shatter the tale to fragments.

—**James Baldwin**

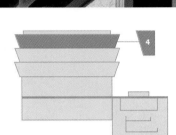

TAKING THE STAGE

Through their achievements in the dramatic arts, African Americans have broken barriers, enriched American culture, and inspired audiences around the world. Over time, the roles that black artists played on the stage and screen reflected changing aspirations, struggles, and realities for black people in American society. As African Americans gained more freedom to express their creative talents and visions, they used the power of performance to fuel social change.

Taking the Stage explores the history of African Americans on the stage and screen, to celebrate their creative achievements, demonstrate their cultural impact, and illuminate their struggles for artistic freedom and equal representation. At the entrance to the gallery, you are greeted by a collage of more than one hundred portraits of artists and entertainers, reflecting the diversity of African American performance from the 1800s to the present. The exhibition then unfolds in three main sections: theater, film, and television.

Spotlights illuminate famous artists of the stage and screen at the entrance to *Taking the Stage*.

A case devoted to Broadway features props and costumes from the plays of August Wilson and the musical sensation *The Wiz*.

Theater

From literary dramas to Broadway musicals, vaudeville to ballet, African Americans have transformed the theatrical stage through diverse approaches to performance. Black actors have challenged typecasting and taken on new roles. Black playwrights, directors, designers, and choreographers have crafted innovative forms of storytelling and new stories about the African American experience. While some artist-activists led efforts to diversify the mainstream theater, others worked to develop an independent theater for the black community.

Objects that illuminate the history of African Americans on the theatrical stage include an 1857 broadside advertising a performance by Ira Aldridge, the first American actor to achieve fame overseas; and a poster from a 1945 production by the American Negro Theatre, founded in Harlem in 1940 to foster the careers of black actors, directors, and playwrights.

The diverse voices and visions that African American artists brought to Broadway are evoked by fantastical costumes designed by Geoffrey Holder for *The Wiz* (1975); the piano from August Wilson's Pulitzer-winning play

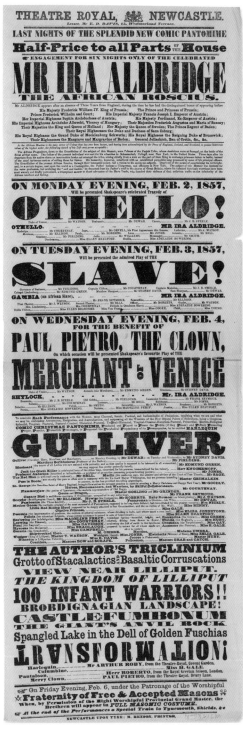

The Piano Lesson (1990); and three dresses from the production of Ntozake Shange's groundbreaking feminist choreopoem, *for colored girls who have considered suicide/ when the rainbow is enuf* (1976). An area devoted to the topic of theatrical dance features a case study on the Dance Theatre of Harlem, the company founded by Arthur Mitchell in 1969 to challenge the racist convention that black dancers could not perform classical ballet; and a video highlighting the work of modern dance choreographers such as Alvin Ailey, Katherine Dunham, Pearl Primus, and Bill T. Jones.

An 1857 broadside advertises a performance by Ira Aldridge at the Theatre Royal in Newcastle, England.

Posters, costumes, and clips reflect changes in Black Hollywood from the early motion picture era to the present.

Film

The history of African Americans in film dates back to the silent era and encompasses all aspects of moviemaking, on screen and behind the scenes. Black artists working in Hollywood struggled to break into the movie industry and break out of stereotyped roles, a struggle that has continued into the twenty-first century. Meanwhile, black independent filmmakers created movies that catered to black audiences and brought more positive and wide-ranging images of African American life to the silver screen.

A spectacular display of costumes reflects the different and changing roles black actors have played in Hollywood films. These include a green velvet dress worn by Lena Horne in the 1943 musical *Stormy Weather*; a fur coat worn by Max Julien in the 1973 blaxploitation-era classic *The Mack*; a boxing robe and trunks worn by Denzel Washington as Rubin "Hurricane" Carter

in *The Hurricane* (1999); and a dress worn by Lupita Nyong'o in her Oscar-winning role in *12 Years a Slave* (2013). Other objects represent pioneering work behind the scenes, such as: two Academy Awards won by sound engineer Russell Williams II; and equipment and clothing used by members of the Black Stuntmen's Association. Looking beyond Hollywood, a display of posters and lobby cards represents various "race films" that were produced for black audiences during the era of segregation. At a time when Hollywood restricted black actors to musical or servant roles, these independent films depicted a wide range of black characters and experiences, from middle-class families to gangsters and cowboys. The most successful black filmmaker of this era was Oscar Micheaux, who wrote, directed, and produced approximately forty films between 1919 and 1948; the display includes a poster from his 1931 film, *The Exile*, which explored the taboo subject of interracial romance and was the first black-cast feature film with sound.

Television

By bringing a stage into the nation's living rooms, television offered new opportunities for African Americans to shape popular culture and work for social change. But many TV shows, including early 1950s sitcoms like *Amos 'n' Andy* and *Beulah*, reflected the persistence of racial stereotypes and discrimination in the entertainment industry. As black artists and activists challenged negative representations and sought more control over the airwaves, they struggled to adjust the picture to include a broader definition of African American identity and experience.

Highlights in this section include a display of costumes from TV shows of the 1960s and 1970s, from *Julia* and *The Flip Wilson Show* to *Good Times* and *The Jeffersons*; a dynamic video presentation, "Changing the Channels," which explores changing representations of African Americans on television from the 1950s to the 2010s; a story about *Jet* magazine's "Television" page, which served as an alternative TV guide for the black community for more than fifty years; and a 1972 NAACP Image Award presented to television director Mark Warren, who was also the first black director to win an Emmy Award. On the other side of the gallery, a section explores the connection between television and stand-up comedy, featuring the stories of black comedians such as Redd Foxx, Dick Gregory, and Jackie "Moms" Mabley, who successfully crossed over from segregated nightclubs into mainstream American culture during the 1960s through performances on network variety shows like *Ed Sullivan* as well as hit comedy albums.

Pioneering shows like *The Flip Wilson Show* and *Good Times* transformed the way African Americans appeared on TV.

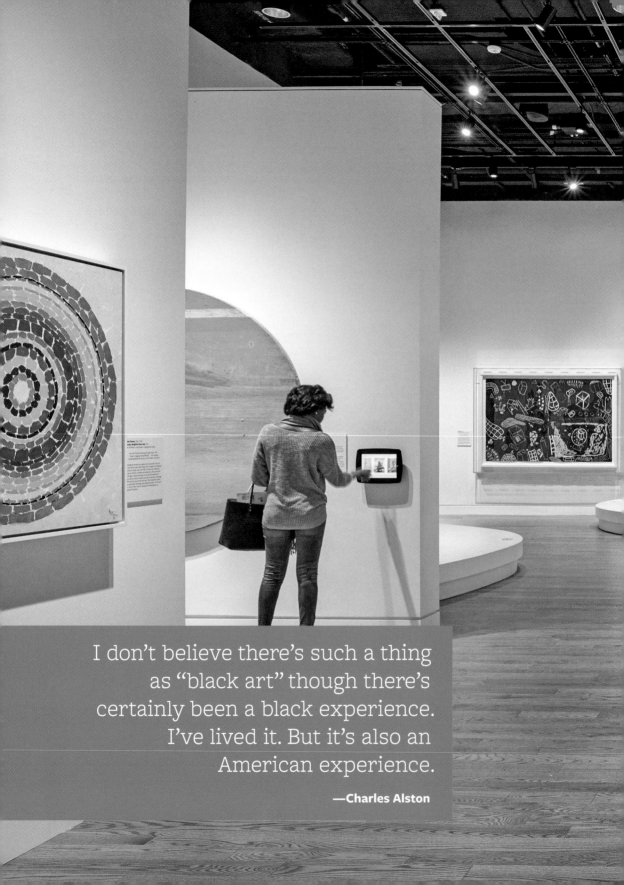

I don't believe there's such a thing as "black art" though there's certainly been a black experience. I've lived it. But it's also an American experience.

—**Charles Alston**

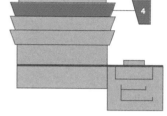

VISUAL ART AND THE AMERICAN EXPERIENCE

At the National Museum of African American History and Culture, the visual arts play a vital role in illuminating the American experience through an African American lens. Paintings, sculptures, and works on paper offer insight into how artists viewed and interpreted their world. While these works may delight and stimulate our senses, each, in its own way, also contributes to our understanding of an era.

Visual Art and the American Experience illustrates the critical role that artists of African descent played in shaping the history of American art. The exhibition is organized into seven thematic sections and also includes a small changing exhibit gallery. Interactive media stations located throughout the exhibition invite you to delve more deeply into the artworks on view.

Sculpted of wood from President Obama's inauguration platform, Jefferson Pinder's *Mothership (Capsule)*, 2009, center, is in a section titled "New Materials, New Worlds."

The World Around Us

Elements of the environment—whether found in nature or crafted by human beings—can serve as inspiration for artists. Painters such as Grafton Tyler Brown (*View of Lake Okanagan*, 1882), Robert Duncanson (*Robbing the Eagle's Nest*, 1856), and Hale Woodruff (*Untitled (Green Landscape)*, ca. 1969–70) focused on the vastness and majesty of the outdoors, perhaps seeing in nature a reflection of the divine. In contrast, Archibald Motley (*The Argument*, 1940) and Joshua Johnson (*Portrait of John Westwood*, ca. 1807–08) were inspired by notions of community and the people they encountered in their lives. Loïs Mailou Jones (*Château d'Olhain, 1947*) and William A. Harper (*Untitled (French Landscape)*, 1905) captured views that reflected their experiences living and working abroad, where many African American artists found greater freedom and acceptance. Others, such as still-life painters Charles Ethan Porter (*Still Life with Roses*, ca. 1885–87) and Pauline Powell Burns (*Violets*, ca. 1890), consciously and painstakingly shaped the elements that defined their world. Through a variety of styles and approaches, these artists' efforts have informed and enriched *our* world.

The Politics of Identity

Identity—the terms by which we define who we are—is central to the way we navigate our lives. But identity is also complex and multifaceted, especially in the United States, where there is often no shorthand to easily define people from so many mixed backgrounds. Some artists have examined the relationship of race to identity, whether viewing it as a source of pride, as in the case of Meta Vaux Warrick Fuller

Meta Vaux Warrick Fuller, *Ethiopia,* ca. 1921.

Joshua Johnson, *Portrait of John Westwood*, ca. 1807–08.

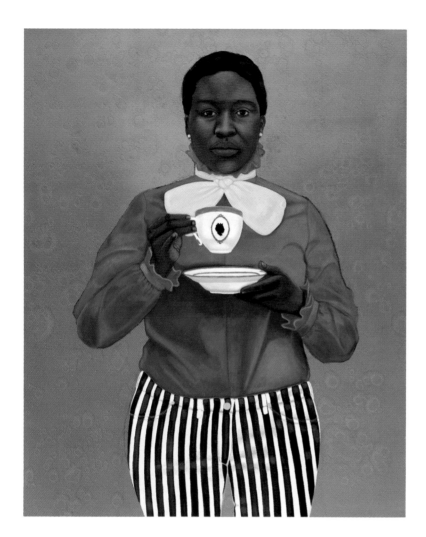

Amy Sherald, *Grand Dame Queenie*, 2013.

(*Ethiopia*, ca. 1921) and Thelma Johnson Streat (*Medicine and Transportation*, ca. 1940), or as a cause of alienation and isolation, as expressed by Hughie Lee-Smith (*Untitled*, ca. 1959–60). Other artists such as Nelson Stevens (Arty, 1970) used portraiture to elevate African American subjects to positions of reverence and respect. Whether we look to the portrait of James Porter (*Self-Portrait,* ca. 1935), a painter, professor, and art historian depicted at his easel with brush and palette in hand, or to Amy Sherald's enigmatic portrait of a young woman sipping tea from a cup adorned with the silhouetted head of a black woman (*Grand Dame Queenie*, 2013), we are reminded that each of us is many things.

The Struggle for Freedom

The history of the United States is one of both triumph and struggle. Americans won freedom and independence from Great Britain in the Revolutionary War, but those privileges did not extend to all. In addition to the historic struggles for religious, racial, and gender equality, many Americans continue to seek solutions to inequalities that remain. The artists here express their political vigilance—for example, Charles Alston (*Walking*, 1958) referencing the Montgomery bus boycott and Alvin Hollingsworth (*Trapped*, 1965) revealing the legacy of redlining, the discriminatory lending practices that kept

Charles Alston, *Walking*, 1958.

urban neighborhoods racially and economically segregated. Artists such as Vincent Smith (*Do-Rag Brother,* 1968) and Carolyn Mims Lawrence (*Uphold Your Men,* ca. 1971) infused their work with a spirit of resistance and solidarity and explored complex dynamics of race, gender, and power. Charles Alston, with his bronze portrait of Martin Luther King Jr. (*Reverend Martin Luther King,* commissioned in 1970), paid tribute to a leader who embodied and advanced the quest for freedom.

African Connections

Americans of African descent define themselves in part by their African heritage and the surviving traditions that enrich both their own lives and those of the larger multicultural society. The paintings of Floyd Coleman (*Shango's Helper,* 1972) and James Phillips (*Sankofa II,* 1997–98) invoke traditional symbols and concepts of Yoruba and Akan people of West Africa to demonstrate the cross-fertilization of American beliefs and those of the African visual culture. Rather than creating an image, Renée Stout (*Ceremonial Object,* 1980) crafted her own sacred object, inspired by artifacts used in African religious rituals, leaving its interpretation to viewers. The link to Africa has also been a source of inspiration for political movements—both for causes in the United States like civil rights and Black Power, and for international action against

the South African apartheid system, as evoked by Howardena Pindell's *Separate But Equal: Apartheid* (1987).

Religion and Spirituality

Themes of religion and spirituality have been common threads in art from its very beginning. Elements of these themes are especially notable in David Driskell's *Behold Thy Son* (1956), inspired by the 1955 murder of fourteen-year-old Emmett Till, and Clementine Hunter's *Black Jesus* (ca. 1985), where there is clear reference to Christianity and the crucifixion of Christ. African American religious traditions have strong roots in Christianity but include other spiritual pathways, including Islam and Judaism, which are also referenced in works displayed in this section of the gallery.

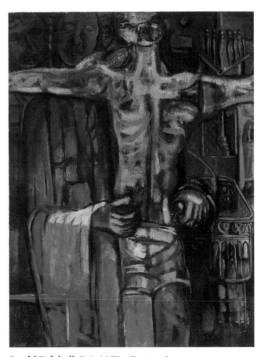

David Driskell, *Behold Thy Son*, 1956.

The Beauty of Color and Form

Traditionally, visual artists have used color and form to make pictures or images readily recognizable—landscapes, figures, animals, or flowers. In the twentieth century, however, some American artists began to experiment with these fundamental elements to create abstract compositions that might or might not have a relationship to objects and scenes in the real world. This approach characterizes the work of such painters as Ed Clark (*The Big Egg,* 1968) and Felrath Hines (*Untitled,* 1978), and sculptor Sargent Claude Johnson (*Dancer,* ca. 1938–40). To achieve their visions, artists employed distinctive compositional techniques, such as the mosaic-style painting of Alma Thomas (*Spring—Delightful Flower Bed,* 1967) and Al Loving's use of torn, cut, and layered rag paper in works like *Red Hook #5* (1993). In liberating themselves from the constraints of conventional aesthetics, many abstract artists found a sense of personal as well as stylistic freedom.

New Materials, New Worlds

Artists are clever and resourceful. When traditional materials like oil paint, acrylic, and plaster are hard to come by, or to work with, or simply do not help achieve the artist's goal, innovation can make success happen. Chakaia Booker (*Urban Mask,* 2001) longed for a material that would be strong, cheap, and durable. Slit and shredded rubber tires turned out to be the solution. When BK Adams envisioned a horse, nothing he could invent worked as well as the discarded bicycle parts, gold foil, and other remnants that came together in *Blue Horse* (2009). Thornton Dial, too, saw an animal in his mind's eye, and it was made of cloth, rope, paint, and discarded carpeting (*Untitled,* 1990s). The work of these artists and others featured here, including Melvin Edwards (*Max Bond Architect* from the series *Lynch Fragments,* 2009), Jefferson Pinder (*Mothership (Capsule),* 2009), and Kevin E. Cole (*Increase Risk with Emotional Faith,* 2008), emphasize the risk-taking and adventurous attitude that brings us new visions and new definitions of what art can be.

Kevin E. Cole, *Increase Risk with Emotional Faith,* 2008.

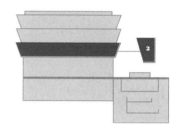

EXPLORE MORE!

Explore More! is an interactive, multifaceted educational space dedicated to helping visitors connect and engage with African American history and culture in ways that expand perspectives, spark curiosity and creativity, and increase knowledge. Located on the museum's second floor, the space is designed to complement and expand on themes and topics presented in the permanent exhibition galleries on the History, Community, and Culture floors. Through the combined use of multimedia technology, exhibits and collections, live performance, and hands-on activities, Explore More! offers a dynamic and personalized museum experience for visitors of all ages.

The Center for African American Media Arts (CAAMA) offers interactive access to the museum's growing photography and film collection.

EXPLORE MORE!

Located on the museum's second floor, Explore More! offers learning opportunities for visitors of all ages through digital interactives, exhibits, hands-on activities, research centers, and classroom programs.

Robert Frederick Smith
Explore Your Family
History Center

Research
Library and
Archives

Transitions
in Freedom
Interactive

Interactive
Gallery

Classrooms

Target
Learning
Center

Earl W. and Amanda
Stafford Center for
African American
Media Arts

In the interactive gallery, visitors can join in a virtual step show and investigate the wreck of a slave ship.

Target Learning Center

At the heart of the Explore More! floor is the Target Learning Center, a 6,000-square-foot interactive gallery with 1,650 square feet of adjoining classrooms. Interactive experiences in the gallery include the Arc, a 30-foot-long curved digital wall populated with objects and stories from the museum's collections, and several exploration stations where you can participate in virtual activities, such as investigating the wreck of the *São José*, the slave ship of the 1700s discovered and documented through the efforts of the Slave Wrecks Project; taking a journey through Jim Crow-era America with help from the *Green Book*, a travel guide for African Americans published by Victor H. Green from the 1930s to the 1960s; and learning the cultural dance form of stepping from members of the professional dance company Step Afrika! Public programs and hands-on learning activities are also regularly offered in the interactive gallery. The classrooms provide flexible spaces for student and teacher programs, workshops, demonstrations, and other group-learning activities.

Robert Frederick Smith Explore Your Family History Center

How does your family's story connect to African American history? In the Robert Frederick Smith Explore Your Family History Center, you can delve into digital resources related to family history, including the Freedmen's Bureau digital archives and genealogical databases; receive expert guidance on how to conduct genealogical research and oral history interviews; see examples of objects from the museum collections relating to family history; and learn how to preserve your own family photographs, documents, and heirlooms. The center also features an interactive digital experience, "Transitions in Freedom," which traces the histories of African American families from slavery to freedom through records from the Freedmen's Bureau and other archival documents, maps, and photographs. Public programs and workshops provide more in-depth information and hands-on learning opportunities related to family history research and preservation.

Earl W. and Amanda Stafford Center for African American Media Arts

Located at the entrance to the Explore More! floor, the Earl W. and Amanda Stafford Center for African American Media Arts (CAAMA) is dedicated to examining the formation of African American history and culture through the media arts, including photography, film, video, and audio recordings. In its space—a dramatic red glass-enclosed "jewel box"—CAAMA offers a regular schedule of changing exhibitions that showcase historical themes and current trends in the media arts. An interactive table and tablet stations provide digital access to the museum's growing collection of visual and aural media. CAAMA also sponsors film series and other public programs, including media digitization and conservation workshops to help visitors preserve their own home movies, photographs, and oral histories.

Research Library and Archives

The NMAAHC Research Library and Archives provides access to resources that support scholarship in African American history, culture, and the African diaspora. The library features a reading room with computer stations, stack space for 11,000 volumes, and electronic, print, and archival resources. An exhibit case next to the entrance features rotating displays of library books and archival materials. The library is open to visiting researchers by appointment; for more information, visit the Smithsonian Libraries website, library.si.edu.

FREEDMEN'S BUREAU RECORDS

The records serve as a bridge to slavery and freedom.... They are the earliest records detailing people who were formerly enslaved. We get a sense of their voice, their dreams.

—HOLLIS GENTRY, Genealogy Specialist

The Hughes Family: This photograph of two enslaved women and their children was taken near Alexandria, Virginia, during the Civil War.

Established by the federal government in March 1865, the Freedmen's Bureau provided services and support to newly emancipated African Americans and their families during the transition from slavery to citizenship. The Bureau also provided aid to poor southern whites who had remained loyal to the Union during the Civil War. Bureau agents operated field offices in fifteen southern and border states, as well as the District of Columbia. The records of the Freedmen's Bureau, spanning from 1865 to 1872, document a wide range of activities—from providing food, clothing, shelter, and medical assistance, to establishing schools, managing confiscated or abandoned lands, negotiating labor contracts, arbitrating disputes, solemnizing marriages, and helping formerly enslaved people reunite with their families.

In 2011, the National Museum of African American History and Culture joined in a collaborative effort with FamilySearch to digitize and index the Freedmen's Bureau records preserved by the National Archives and make them freely accessible to online researchers. Since 2015, when the first set of digitized records was released online, thousands of volunteers have indexed nearly two million records. These records, offering glimpses into people's everyday lives and struggles during this extraordinary time in American history, represent a treasure trove of information for genealogists and historians. To make this information even more accessible, the museum has partnered with the Smithsonian Transcription Center to generate word-by-word transcripts of the individual documents so they can also be searched by keyword. You can learn more about the Freedmen's Bureau records in the Robert Frederick Smith Explore Your Family History Center on the museum's second floor, and on the web at nmaahc.si.edu/explore/initiatives/freedmens-bureau-records. You can also volunteer to help transcribe Freedmen's Bureau records and other historical documents from the museum's collection by visiting the Smithsonian Transcription Center at transcription.si.edu.

CONTINUE THE JOURNEY

The National Museum of African American History and Culture is just one of many sites around Washington, D.C., and across the United States where you can explore the African American experience.

Around the Smithsonian

Several other Smithsonian museums feature collections, exhibitions, and programs that relate to African American history and add other perspectives to the American story. **The National Museum of American History** (Constitution Avenue NW, between 12th and 14th Streets; americanhistory.si.edu) presents exhibitions on a variety of topics, from politics and democracy, religion, and immigration to popular culture, science and technology, and business; a permanent exhibit about the 1960 civil rights sit-in in Greensboro, North Carolina, includes an original section of the Woolworth's lunch counter. The **Smithsonian American Art Museum** (8th and F Streets, NW; americanart.si.edu) has more than two thousand works by African American artists in its collection. The **National Museum of African Art** (950 Independence Avenue SW; africa.si.edu) offers exhibitions and programs that explore African arts and cultures across time and throughout the diaspora. The **National Museum of the American Indian** (4th Street and Independence Avenue, SW; nmai.si.edu) promotes understanding of Native cultures and communities and explores political and cultural interactions between Native peoples and other groups in American society; NMAI partnered with NMAAHC in 2009 to produce a publication and exhibition entitled *Indivisible: African-Native American Lives in the Americas*. The **Anacostia Community Museum** (1901 Fort Place SE; anacostia.si.edu), founded in 1967 to promote educational outreach to the local African American community in Washington, D.C., develops projects, exhibitions, and programs that examine issues of impact to contemporary urban communities.

Around D.C.

In addition to the Lincoln Memorial and the Martin Luther King Jr. Memorial on the National Mall, the **National Park Service** (nps.gov) operates a number of sites related to African American history and culture elsewhere in Washington, D.C., including the African American National Civil War Memorial (1925 Vermont Avenue NW), the Carter G. Woodson Home National Historic Site (1538 9th Street NW; currently closed to the public), the Mary McLeod Bethune Council House National Historic Site (1318 Vermont Avenue NW), and the Frederick Douglass National Historic Site (1411 W Street SE).

The **African American Heritage Trail**, created by Cultural Tourism DC, identifies more than two hundred sites throughout the nation's capital that connect to African American history and culture at the local and national level. A free, self-guided tour booklet, which includes fifteen neighborhood walking tours around the city, is available to download at culturaltourismdc.org.

Around the U.S.

Many guidebooks and websites are available to direct you to African American museums and historic sites located throughout the United States. **BlackPast.org**, the online reference center for African American history, maintains state-by-state listings of African American historic landmarks and museums on its website (blackpast.org). **The Association of African American Museums** (AAAM) is another resource for learning more about museums that focus on the history, art, and culture of people of African descent, both in the United States and around the world, as well as for information about museum employment and professional development opportunities (blackmuseums.org).

GENERAL INFORMATION

Location: The National Museum of African American History and Culture is located on the National Mall at 1400 Constitution Avenue NW, between Madison and Constitution Avenues and 14th and 15th Streets, Washington, D.C. There are two entrances to the museum: one on Madison Avenue and another on Constitution Avenue.

Admission: Free, but timed passes may be required for entry. Please visit the museum website for more information.

Hours: Open daily (except December 25) from 10:00 a.m. to 5:30 p.m.

Museum Website: For information about the museum, including current and upcoming exhibitions, special events, and public programs, visit nmaahc.si.edu.

Information Services: Volunteer Visitor Services Representatives and Docents are available to provide advice and to help navigate the exhibition galleries and all of the various opportunities and services that are part of the museum experience. Printed brochures in English, French, and Spanish are available at the Walmart Welcome Center on the Entry Level.

Mobile App: The NMAAHC Mobile App serves as a complement to the onsite museum experience. Features include stories for families with children, building stories, outdoor stories, and multimedia and augmented reality (AR) experiences, along with museum maps, program schedules, and other visitor information. The app is free and available to download via the museum website. Loaner mobile devices are also available at the museum's Welcome Center.

Tours: Gallery talks led by museum volunteers and other tour opportunities are scheduled on a regular basis. Please visit the museum website for the most current information.

Groups: Groups are welcome at the museum. For information on special offers and tour packages for groups visiting the Smithsonian, see si.edu/Visit/VisitInfoGroups.

Parking: There are no Smithsonian Institution public parking facilities on the National Mall. Free on-street parking for cars and vans on Jefferson Drive and Madison Drive on the National Mall is limited, and the three-hour posted regulations are enforced. Parking is available in nearby commercial lots and garages; for additional information see si.edu/Visit/Maps. For information on bus parking sites, contact the National Park Service Mall Operations Office at 202.426.6841.

Public Transportation: Metrobus and Metrorail, Washington's bus and subway systems, link the city with communities in nearby Maryland and Virginia. Every subway station is equipped with an elevator and/or escalators. For information on Metrobus and Metrorail schedules, as well as parking at Metro stations, call 202.637.7000 (voice) or 202.638.3780 (TTY), or visit the Metro website at wmata.com.

Photography: Still and video photography for noncommercial use only is permitted in the museum and exhibitions, unless otherwise posted. Photography of fine art is prohibited. For the safety of our visitors and collections, the use of tripods, monopods, and selfie sticks is not permitted at any time. To assist with capturing your memories, the museum provides a mobile application with a variety of images from our exhibitions and collections.
Notice: Visitors may be filmed, photographed, or recorded by the Smithsonian for educational and promotional uses, including for posting on the Smithsonian's and other public websites.

Pets: Pets (except service animals) are not permitted in the museum.

Dining: Sweet Home Café, located on the Concourse level, seats 400 people and features a rotating menu of seasonal offerings served at four stations and includes family-friendly options. The stations are organized to showcase traditional African American cuisine from the following U.S. regions: the Northern States, the Agricultural South, the Creole Coast, and the Western Range. Visitors are not allowed to bring food into the museum, and coolers are also not permitted in the museum or on the grounds.

Shopping: The museum store, located on the Entry Level, offers a wide selection of crafts, publications, recordings, and other merchandise that illustrate the richness and diversity of the African American experience.

The Oprah Winfrey Theater: The museum's 350-seat auditorium is used for public programs and special events during and after museum hours. For the current program schedule, visit the museum website.

Accessibility Information: The museum is accessible to visitors with disabilities. A limited number of manual wheelchairs are available free of charge on a first-come, first-served basis. Open captioning is included in all exhibition videos. For more information on specific resources and accommodations, visit si.edu/Accessibility/VisitorsWithDisabilities or contact the Smithsonian Accessibility Program at 202.633.2921 (voice), access@si.edu (email).

The porch and reflecting pool are signature features of the museum's south entrance.

Photography Credits

NATIONAL MUSEUM OF AFRICAN AMERICAN HISTORY AND CULTURE: 2-3: Alan Karchmer **6:** Michael Barnes/Smithsonian Institution **7:** Alan Karchmer **8-9:** Alan Karchmer **10:** 2016.74, Gift from the Ball-Hoagland family in honor of Robert Ball **11:** Alan Karchmer **12:** 2013.201.1.54 **15:** Michael Barnes/Smithsonian Institution **16:** 2011.160.9, Gift of David A. Lowrance **17:** Alan Karchmer **20:** 2008.15.2, Gift of Dr. Patricia Heaston **21:** 2011.30.2, Gift of Linda and Artis Cason; 2012-93.1-.2, Gift of Ina Mae LaRue **22-23:** Alan Karchmer **24:** Photograph by Martin Stupich **25:** Alan Karchmer **26:** Michael Barnes/Smithsonian Institution **27:** Alan Karchmer **28:** Alan Karchmer **29:** 2016.147, © Sam Gilliam, 2016 **29:** 2015.255, Gift of Richard and Laura Parsons, © Romare Bearden Foundation/Licensed by VAGA **31:** Eric Long **32:** 2011.69 **34-35:** Eric Long **37:** 2013.46.1 **37:** 2011.28, Gift of Maurice A. Person and Noah and Brooke Porter **37:** 2012.4 **38:** Eric Long **38-39:** Eric Long **40:** Alex Jamison **41:** 2009.14.1 **43:** 2016.168 **44:** Alan Karchmer **45:** 2010.14 **45:** 2014.25, Gift of Elaine E. Thompson, in memory of Joseph Trammell, on behalf of his direct descendants **46:** Alex Jamison **48:** 2009.50.39, Gift of Charles L. Blockson **48-49:** Eric Long **50:** 2014.115.9, Gift of the Garrison Family in memory of George Thompson Garrison **51:** 2012.133 **52-53:** Eric Long **53:** 2013.168.1, Gift of the Family of William Beverly Nash **54-55:** Alan Karchmer **56:** 2013.208.2a-k, Gift of Dr. and Mrs. T.B. Boyd, III and R.H. Boyd Publishing Corporation **56:** 2006.1, Gift of Quinn Chapel African Methodist Episcopal Church, Chicago, Illinois **57:** 2012.117.1ab, Gift of Carlotta Walls LaNier **57:** 2015.226.2, Donated by the International Civil Rights Center & Museum, Greensboro, NC **59:** Alex Jamison **60:** 2010.2.2a-d **61:** Alex Jamison **62:** 2012.3.1 **63:** 2011.73.1, Gift of the Descendants of Garfield Logan, In Honor of Philip Henry Logan **64:** 2012.46.73.2 **65:** 2011.76.7a-d, Donated by Halimah Mohammed Ali, granddaughter of the Hon. Elijah Mohammad and Clara Muhammad **66:** 2012.86 **67:** 2013.205.1, Gift of the Louis J. Beasley Family **68-69:** Eric Long **69:** 2007.3.1ab, Gift of the Black Fashion Museum founded by Lois K. Alexander-Lane **70:** 2010.71.3, Gift from the Trumpauer-Mulholland Collection; 2013.138a-c, Gift of the Family of Rev. Norman C. "Jim" Jimerson and Melva Brooks Jimerson **71:** 2011.53 **73:** Alan Karchmer; Eric Long **74:** Alan Karchmer **75:** Alan Karchmer **76-77:** Alan Karchmer

78: 2015.177, Dress designed by Tracy Reese and wron by the First lady in connection with the 50th Anniversary of the March on Washington **78:** 2013.123.4 **79:** 2016.7.7, Gift of Oprah Winfrey **79:** 2012.136 **80-81:** 2012.83.6, Gift of the Pirkle Jones Foundation, ©2011 Pirkle Jones Foundation **82:** 2011.159.3.43, Gift from Dawn Simon Spears and Alvin Spears, Sr. **82-83:** 2012.110, Gift of Vincent DeForest **83:** 2014.252 © Platt Poster Co. **84:** 2011.109.13.8, Gift from the Trumpauer-Mulholland Collection **85:** 2010.30 **86:** 2010.2.1abc **88:** 2015.149, Gift from the Southern University System, Southern University and A&M College, University of Louisiana System, Grambling State University **88:** 2013.213.9 **89:** 2014.29.1 **89:** 2013.70.1, Gift of First A.M.E. Church of Los Angeles **90-91:** Alan Karchmer **92:** 2011.88.6ab, Gift of Rabbi Capers Funnye and the Beth Shalom B'nai Zaken Ethiopian Hebrew Congregation **93:** 2013.70.1, Gift of First A.M.E. Church of Los Angeles; 2014.213.2, Gift of the Gates Moresi family **94:** Alex Jamison **95:** 2013.90.2.1-.2, Gift of Pauline Brown Payne **96:** 2013.133.2.2, Gift of the Historical Society of Washington, DC, and the Alpha Kappa Alpha Sorority, Inc.; 2013.71.1abc, Gift of Worshipful Prince Hall Grand Lodge of Massachusetts **97:** 2013.104.2ab, Gift of Charles Thomas Lewis; 2013.2018.1a-e, Gift of Dr. and Mrs. T.B. Boyd, III and R.H. Boyd Publishing Corporation **98:** 2009.1.5, Gift of Robert Galbraith, © 1987 Robert Galbraith; 2013.46.19 **99:** 2013.62.1, Gift of Mrs. Mary Churchwell and Dr. Kevin Churchwell and Mrs. Gloria Churchwell 100-101: Alan Karchmer **102-103:** Alan Karchmer **104:** Eric Long **105:** 2013.142, Donated by Erma Johnson, Felicia Taylor, Katherine Taylor, and Ronald Johnson; 2007.1.37.1 **107:** 2012.96.1-.5, Gift of Scott Ellsworth **107-108:** Eric Long **108:** 2014.312.19.1-.2, Gift of Oprah Winfrey 109: Eric Long **110:** 2013.213.7; 2010.6.47, Gift from Mae Reeves and her children, Donna Limerick and William Mincey, Jr. **111:** Eric Long; 2013.213.6 **112-113:** Alan Karchmer **114:** 2011.4.2ab **115:** 2012.34.1.1abc, Gift of the Family of Frances Sampson Mask; 2011.108.9.1, gift of Gina R. McVey, granddaughter **116:** 2015.97.24 **117:** 2011.146.1.5abc, Gift of Alice Calberb F. Royal; 2014.243.6, Gift of Maj. Gen. Charles F. Bolden Jr., USMC (Ret) **118:** 2013.165.1.1ab-.3, Gift of Ray R. and Patricia A.D. Charlton in memory of Cornelius H. Charlton **118-119:** Alan Karchmer **120-121:** Alan Karchmer **122:** Alex Jamison **123:** 2015.231.2; 2014.30.2 **124:** 2014.194.1 **124-125:** Alex Jamison; 2013.120.9 **126:** 2009.27.5; 2010.19.1 **127:** Alan Karchmer **128:** 2011.137.2, Donation of Charles E. Berry **130:** 2012.89, Gift of B.K. Adams – I

Gift of B.K. Adams – I AM ART, © B.K. Adams – I AM ART; 2011.50.2, Gift of Soul Train Holdings, LLC, © Soul Train Holdings, LLC **131:** 2013.145.1-2; 2013.118.32; 2007.3.21, Gift of the Black Fashion Museum founded by Lois K. Alexander-Lane **132-133:** Alan Karchmer **134:** 2008.18, Gift of Juan Garcia Salazar **135:** 2014.322, © Estate of Art Smith; 2008.11.1ab, © Phillip Simmons **136:** 2014.201, © Kenya **137:** 2014.218.1, Gift of Dooky Chase's Restaurant and Chef Leah Chase **138-139:** Alan Karchmer **140:** 2012.125.50ab, Gift of Charley Pride **141:** 2010.23.2ab **142:** 2013.59.3ab, Gift of Antoine "Fats" Domino; 2014.97.2 **143:** 2013.8, Gift of the Celia Cruz Knight Estate **144:** 2015.187, Gift of Mark James; 2014.139.1-.2a, Gift of Maureen Yancy **145:** 2008.7.4 **146:** 2011.83.6, Gift of Love to the planet **146-147:** Eric Long **148:** 2011.19 **149:** Alex Jamison **150:** 2008.16.1-.3 **151:** 2014.27.2, Gift of Ginette DePreist in memory of James DePreist **152:** Alan Karchmer **153:** Alex Jamison **154-155:** Eric Long **156-157:** Eric Long **157:** 2011.57.44 **158:** Eric Long **159:** Eric Long **160-161:** Alan Karchmer **162:** 2010.25ab; 2013.242.1, Gift of the Fuller Family, © Meta Vaux Warrick Fuller **163:** 2013.20, © Amy Sherald **164:** 2007.2, Gift of Sydney Smith Gordon, © Charles Alston Estate; 2009.7, © David C. Driskell **165:** 2009.12, Gift of Greg and Yolanda Head, © Kevin Cole **166-167:** Alex Jamison **168:** Alan Karchmer **170:** 2014.174.8 **173:** Alan Karchmer **175:** Alan Karchmer

OTHER: 14: Photo by Paul Morse/White House **19:** Courtesy of Clearly Innovative **30:** Courtesy of Restaurant Associates **42:** Courtesy of Iziko Museums **43:** Courtesy of Iziko Museums

Text Credits

page 10, paragraph one: "Fifty Years," *Afro-American*, October 2, 1915, page 4

page 10, paragraph two: National Memorial Association. *Design of the proposed national memorial building to commemorate the heroic deeds of Negro soldiers and sailors who fought in all the Nation's wars*, ca. 1926. W. E. B. Du Bois Papers (MS 312). Special Collections and University Archives, University of Massachusetts Amherst Libraries

page 10, paragraph three: Senate Joint Resolution 132, Public Resolution No. 107, 70th Cong., 2nd sess., March 4, 1929

page 13, paragraph two: Robert L. Wilkins, Esq., "The Forgotten Museum," July 31, 2002, page 16

Acknowledgments

We would like to thank National Museum of African American History and Culture director Lonnie Bunch, deputy director Kinshasha Holman Conwill, members of the museum's curatorial staff, and other individuals who provided information and images, reviewed portions of the manuscript, and otherwise offered support for this publication: Abigail Benson, Nancy Bercaw, Michael Biddle, Nicole Bryner, Timothy Anne Burnside, Lynn Chase, Shauna Collier, Rhea Combs, Laura Coyle, Spencer Crew, Lynn Ellington, Mary Elliott, Rex Ellis, Tuliza Fleming, Princess Gamble, Paul Gardullo, Hollis Gentry, Joanne Hyppolite, Cheryl Johnson, Kaitlyn Leaf, Minda Logan, Albert Lukas, Deborah Mack, Kathleen McSweeney, Michèle Gates Moresi, Fleur Paysour, Allison Prabhu, William Pretzer, Dwandalyn Reece, Douglas Remley, Tulani Salahu-Din, Krewasky Salter, Brenda Sanchez, Jacquelyn Serwer, Bryan Sieling, Auntaneshia Staveloz, Kevin Strait, Damion Thomas, Selma Thomas, Esther Washington, Tsione Wolde-Michael, Michelle Wilkinson, and Allison Willcox.

Sunlight filtering through the patterned panels of the Corona illuminates the four-story atrium on the west side of the museum.

This book may be purchased for educational, business, or sales promotional use. For information, please write: Special Markets Department, Smithsonian Books, P. O. Box 37012, MRC 513, Washington, DC 20013

Published by Smithsonian Books
Director: Carolyn Gleason
Production Editor: Christina Wiginton
Creative Director: Jody Billert
Editorial Assistant: Jaime Schwender

National Museum of African American History and Culture
Director: Lonnie G. Bunch III
Deputy Director: Kinshasha Holman Conwill
Writer: Kathleen M. Kendrick
Publications Team: Michèle Gates Moresi, Laura Coyle, and Douglas Remley

Smithsonian Photographers: Alex Jamison and Eric Long assisted by Alana Donocoff, Leah Jones, and Ben Sullivan

Architectural Photography: Alan Karchmer

Produced by Potomac Global Media in collaboration with Toucan Books, Ltd.
Kevin Mulroy, Publisher, Potomac Global Media, LLC
Ellen Dupont, Managing Director, Toucan Books, Ltd.
John Andrews, Editor; Marion Dent, Proofreader;
Leah Germann, Art Direction & Design; Ed Merritt, Floorplans

Library of Congress Cataloging-in-Publication Data

Names: Kendrick, Kathleen M. | National Museum of African American History and Culture (U.S.)
Title: Official guide to the Smithsonian National Museum of African American History and Culture / National Museum of African American History and Culture ; Kathleen M. Kendrick.
Description: Washington, D.C. : Smithsonian Books, 2017. | Includes index.
Identifiers: LCCN 2016038059 | ISBN 9781588345936 (paperback)
Subjects: LCSH: National Museum of African American History and Culture (U.S.)--Guidebooks. | BISAC: TRAVEL / United States / South / South Atlantic (DC, DE, FL, GA, MD, NC, SC, VA, WV). | TRAVEL / Museums, Tours, Points of Interest.
Classification: LCC E185.53.W3 N387 2017 | DDC 975.3--dc23 LC record available at https://lccn.loc.gov/2016038059

Manufactured in China, not at government expense
22 21 20 19   6 5 4

For permission to reproduce illustrations appearing in this book, please correspond directly with the owners of the works, as seen on pp. 174–175. Smithsonian Books does not retain reproduction rights for these images individually, or maintain a file of addresses for sources.